£4.50

We thought we'd start with a bang!

THE LIFE TIME BOOK OF THE SUBURBS

Gathering harvest in the suburbs.

An enthralling new documentary library from the creators of *The Illustrated History of Household Cleaners*, *Great Caravan Parks of the World* and *Scenic Wonders of Belgium*.

Did you know

- ⁹⁄₁₀ths of the world's surface is covered with suburbs.
- The most popular street name is 'street'.
- Suburbs were invented by the Mesopotamians.
- There are over nine million acres of grass verge in the South East of England, not including Hove.
- The suburbs are an area around a town centre but not quite in the country.

Snow in the suburbs

From the dawn of time, Man has always sought his own hidey-hole, and a way of covering its exterior with an effective and inexpensive material having low maintenance costs.

Now, in the *Life Time Book of the Suburbs* you can experience the world of Flowering Cherry, Dimplex and Cordula Aluminium Exterior Shutters.

A beautiful woman of the suburbs.

Another beautiful woman of the suburbs.

What draws the teeming hordes back to their modest semi-detached villas as night falls over Ruislip?

Why are there always five shoe shops and no newsagent in the Parade?

Who invented the wrought-iron plant holder?

What is the big appeal of the Ford Escort?

Fresh and exciting, lively and authoritative: through this new series you will discover the explosive history of Man's urge to be leafy.

SOME FAMOUS PEOPLE OF THE SUBURBS:

NIGEL DEMPSTER	MICK JAGGER
ALAN ALDA	NICHOLAS COLERIDGE
PETER STRINGFELLOW	COLIN MCABE
BEN ELTON	

'I'm dead,' says T.V. Personality, John Betjeman (Picture), 'but if I had been alive, I'd have been predictably full of enthusiasm for any tacky book about the suburbs.'

THE SEVEN WONDERS OF THE ANCIENT SUBURBS

1. The Hanging Baskets of Beckenham. **2.** The Great Recreation Ground and Sports Complex of Cheops. **3.** The Intersection of Roads. And four others which you can probably make up yourself.

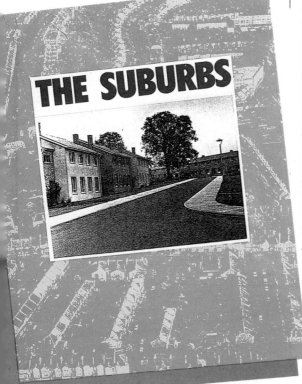

THE SUBURBS

Part of Crouch End

Through the medium of this magnificent and tumultuous book you will experience the core of what has become known the world over as the bookshelf-filling phenomenon.

It builds week by week into a row of volumes that will look truly magnificent next to the photo of Maureen getting married.

EACH HANDSOME VOLUME CONTAINS:

- Paper.
- Photographs so rare that not even we have seen them before we put them in this book.
- Separately numbered pages.
- Printed words, tidily arranged in sentences and paragraphs.
- Diagrams and things.

£45.00

E'S A FRIEND OF YOURS . . . .

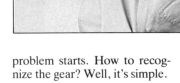

. . . and a fellow policeman, and you notice he's smoking what could be cannabis. What do you do? Do you pretend you haven't noticed and look in the other direction? NO! Not unless in the other direction Brigette Nielson is going skinny dipping. Do you say, 'Hey, please don't do that in front of me'? NO! He'll just say, 'Piss off and mind your own business.' Do you say, 'I'm sorry, I'm going to have to arrest you'? NO! Not unless you know he's got plenty of cash on him and is likely to bribe you. Or do you give him a silly hand-shake and say, 'Mmm that smells like real good gear, man! Where did you get it?' YES. Then it's a career in the Metropolitan Police for you.

A career in the Metropolitan Police opens up untold opportunities for the bright young man or woman on the make. You'll have occasion to meet, socialize and have your photograph taken with top showbiz personalities and violent criminals. (In some cases these are the same.) Obviously there is the odd disadvantage eg. occasionally you're going to be at the same parties as Barbara Windsor. But look on the bright side: complete strangers will be constantly rushing up to you, offering you friendly little tokens of their esteem... like backhanders, cars, unlimited free building materials, clothes, casual sex, booze, hi-fi stereos, high quality porn (and not that bland stuff you get pretending to be health and fitness magazines with lots of pictures of page-three girls with their nipples Tipp-Exed out and the labia air-brushed to non-existence or endless black and white photos of fat naturists with wrinkled willies and saggy wives... no, I'm talking about real nasty stuff... the sort of stuff you can't get in the shops... well, of course you can't, coz we've confiscated it all) and, of course, drugs. Now, this is where the problem starts. How to recognize the gear? Well, it's simple.

Cocaine: A whitish powder; fine or crumbly or crystalline. An up-market combination of hay-fever and diarrhoea, but it is said to improve your chances of becoming a snooker star.

Cannabis Resin: Blackish, brownish, yellowish, sticky substance. It has a characteristic colour... sometimes black, sometimes brown, sometimes yellow. It has a characteristic stickiness. Smoked or eaten, it makes you giggle at first, then it makes you cry, and then it puts you into a sound sleep for days. Rather like watching the *Eurovision Song Contest*.

Marijuana: Indian hemp. Nickname 'Grass'. Looks like grass. When burning it smells like burning grass. Usually smoked in cigarettes, it makes the taker imagine he is lying in the garden while his next-door neighbour is burning the grass from his newly cut lawn.

JOIN THE METROPOLITAN POLICE TODAY

SPOT THE DIFFERENCE

The two High Streets illustrated are 500 miles apart. All you have to do is to spot ten differences between the two drawings of them to justify ever travelling between the two towns.

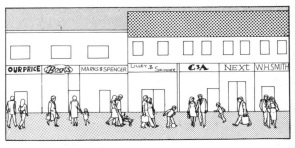

PARIS SNATCH

LE PRINCE CHARLES EST DIVORCÉ DE LADY DI POUR SE MARIER AVEC UN OAK ARBRE

par Pierre Tory

LA PRINCESSE MARGARET EST UNE ALIEN DE L'OUTER-ESPACE

par le Pied Homme de Balmoral

LES 3 CORGIS DE LA REINE ELIZABETH SONT MOURANT DE AIDS

L'histoire étonnant d'une Madame en Attendante, Alison Malcolm

LE PALAIS DE BUCKINGHAM EST VENDU AU RUPERT MURDOCH

exclusif de Paul Pied

ANDY ET FERGIE FONT L'AMOUR 10 FOIS LA NUIT

par witness d'oeil Nigel D'Empster

LE PRINCE EDWARD EST UN THÉ-GARÇON POUR UN HOMM QUI ÉCRIT MAUVAIS MUSICALS POUR LES IDIOTS

par L'Équipe Insight

Three-day sale of the
DUCHESS OF WINDSOR'S
Kitchen Utensils.

Being the entire contents of Her Grace's kitchen, pantry and sink tidy.

To include:

A handsome solid silver Waffle Iron by Garraps of Bond Street.

Massive Fabergé Vacuum Flask in wipe-clean faux chintz with inlaid mahogany and rosewood lift-grip.

The Winter Pic-Nic Basket and matching Cooler Bag. Formerly the property of the Tsar of all the Russias.

Rare plasticated Pinafore decorated with rough impression of female semi-clad nude body in '*bra and panties*' by Coco Chanel.

A good ivory-handled Potato Masher.

An elegant ruby and sapphire Egg Coddler in the shape of the Prince of Wales' Feathers by Askey's of London (*1938.*)

A pair of carved satinwood Gherkin Tongs.

A magnificent solid platignum Tin Opener, the handles decorated with Emeralds and Seed Pearls in form of French Bulldogs. (*Stiff and Kink's, London 1954.*)

A splendid miniature porcelain Spoon Rest, decorated with views of the Rhondda Valley and inscribed with '*We'll Keep a Welcome in the Hillside*' (*Slightly chipped.*)

Rare garnet-encrusted Melon Scoop engraved with contemporary armorials in a 'crossed Windsor-knots' cartouche.

An unusual four-foot high free-standing majolica blackamoor serving lad Soda-Stream Dispenser.

Very good small sandalwood and inlaid ivory Fondue Set. (*Unused.*)

Tin oblong salver, inscribed '*Take Skegness, it's so Bracing*'.

Sundry Whisks in precious metals.

Early Tiffany Roasting Thermometer.

Superb ormolu and ebony Kitchen-Towel Holder. (*Empty.*)

Unique Sèvres enamelled porcelain Chicken Brick.

A good white metal combined Potato Peeler and Cocoa Whisk by Mosiman's of London.

Very rare hexagonal Waterford Crystal Musical Cookie Jar. Plays '*Bess, You is My Woman Now*' on opening (*some notes missing*).

An elegant mother-of-pearl inlaid Palais Royale amboyna wood Necessaire and Tea-Towel Magi-Grip.

Very fine non-stick terracotta Sauce Warmer with jute and silver base.

Cartier diamond-studded Garlic Press.

A pair of solid gold Spaghetti Forks with inlaid mother-of-pearl easi-wipe handle.

A fine George III silver Jelly Mould in the shape of an infant rabbit rampant.

Sundry Tea-towels by Hermes, Jacquard and Issey Miyake.

Part of a set of Measuring Spoons.

Assorted jewel-encrusted Forks, Steak Mallets, Basting Spoons etc.

CHRISTIE'S
LONDON NEW YORK CHELMSFORD

WORD TRACKING

How many words of three letters or more can you find by tracking from one square to the next, going up, down, sideways or diagonally in order, without going through the same letter square more than once in any one word?

Sorry, no foreign words are allowed.

A maximum of ten words can be found, including the hidden nine-letter word. You have ten minutes.

O	Y	B
X	C	L
G	S	U

Answers at bottom of page.

▶ SCRATCH AREA ◀

£6,100 to be **WON!**

Rub the squares with the side of a coin to reveal the hidden pictures

- 4 cherries pays £5,000
- 3 bluebells pays £1,000
- 2 sheep pays £100
- 2 eyes and a nose means you have just scratched through to the next page

---

WORDPLAY

Can you change <u>DIALECTOLOGIST</u> to <u>CONJUNCTIVITIS</u> in 5 moves, changing only one letter in each move?

Answer at bottom of page.

A GUIDE TO ACT
CHILD

BY GRIFF RHYS JONES

INTRODUCTION

Apart from the fact that Mike Smith appears in countless TV shows there can be few mysteries as baffling and miraculous as that of childbirth. Ever since the dawn of shagging, babies have been born. Traditionally it is the woman who gets pregnant. She then begins a long, hard struggle to find the man who made her pregnant and who has inexplicably left the country. The twentieth century has seen the woman playing an increasingly passive role in the birth of her child. She just lies down and lets the doctors get on with it. Just like when she got pregnant in the first place. But modern thinkers assert that women (and men) should eschew medical science and go back to having babies in a natural way like they do in the desert and in the bush. The basic idea behind this is to make men hang around the labour wards for hours on end supporting the woman as she squats and generally feeling the pain and tedium of birth when they could be in the boozer smoking cigars and drinking champagne and generally being congratulated by their mates on being such a big, throbbing, fertile hunk even though he's only had it off once with his wife in the last year and that was because West Ham had avoided relegation and he thought she was somebody else.

THE MEN CAN HELP OUT

LISA HERE LOOKS GREAT EVEN THOUGH SHE IS NEARLY TEN SECONDS PREGNANT

THE POSITIONS

In an active natural birth the woman can sit or squat. The partner can be of assistance here by supporting the squatting woman or by grabbing her round the neck and standing on a table and vigorously shaking her up and down. If baby doesn't come out after that then he's probably not coming out anyway and you might as well go back down the boozer where they'll be on the 217th chorus of 'For He's a Jolly Good Fellow'.

E AND NATURAL
BIRTH

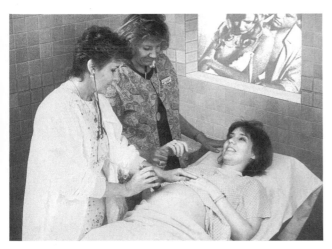

SEX DURING PREGNANCY CAN BE EXCITING RIGHT UP TILL THE LAST MINUTE.

THE ENVIRONMENT
A lot of women nowadays opt to have their baby born under water but this can have unforeseen drawbacks (see fig).

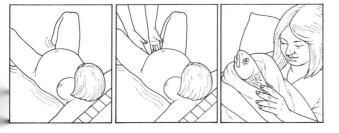

THE PLACENTA
Soon after the birth of a child the placenta or afterbirth appears. This is a round, flat, squashy, gristly piece of meat. If you've had a particularly ugly child, the afterbirth often makes you think you've had twins. The placenta is rich in nutrients and high in protein. Some cultures consider the placenta a culinary delicacy, though in the West we consider this rather distasteful and the only satisfactory way to use it in the dining-room is to put in on a piece of round bread and serve it to your vegetarian friends, telling them that it's a cheese and tomato pizza.

THE JOY OF THE PLACENTA

BREAST FEEDING
After pregnancy breasts get very big indeed and breast feeding is most important. Breasts should be fed three times a day: usually peanuts, chopped fruit and bacon rind will suffice.
It's quite common for a large pair of tits to peck holes in tops of milk bottles and suck the cream out. This can be prevented by putting a bra over the bottles. For more information about what a tit likes to eat see *My Favourite Food* by Keith Floyd.

slow life

The magazine for the get up and go traveller on British Busways, the World's Favourite Tramline

Queen to Open Exciting New Bus Development

On Thursday 4th May, Queen Elizabeth II will formally open the brand new bus shelter on the north side of Notting Hill Gate.

All Wesbound buses on routes 52, 28, 37 and 19B will be transferred to the new combined stop and shelter outside ZACCO's mini-market, making it the busiest non-international bus alighting and boarding point in the world.

The shelter is a joint development of the London Transport Engineering Department and O'Donahue & Mulville (Shepherds Bush) Ltd, builders.

It is constructed from traditional shelter materials – reinforced aluminium, toughened glass and corrugated

WHAT THE BUS CONDUCTOR IS WEARING

JASPER CONRAN'S ROUTEMASTER
New-look Route 31 Combat Uniform

Artfully sculpted cap

Three-day stubble

Rhino-hair necklace

Regulation jacket three sizes too small

Bus conductor badge

Milk monitor badge

Sid Vicious badge

LNER train spotters' badge

I survived Route 85 T-shirt

'The Zinger' extra loud ticket machine

Spare ticket rolls

'Good Boy' dog-collar

Identity bracelet

One black leather glove

Aztec death skull ring

Money bag

Luger 2411 automatic pistol

Ex-Mexican Government Army Surplus Bandolier

Worn and faded Levi 501's

Reebok trainers

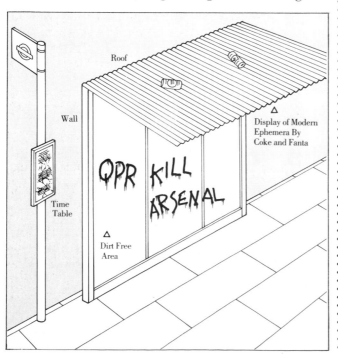

Roof

Wall

Display of Modern Ephemera By Coke and Fanta

QPR KILL ARSENAL

Time Table

Dirt Free Area

iron – but it does have some striking and innovative features:

The shelter has a 25-foot unsupported roof span. At least, it has been unsupported since vandals kicked away its pillars the day after it was put up.

The timetables for the various routes are displayed in a striking 'crazed glass' display cabinet on the bus-stop post where they can be rained on. Incidentally, all four timetables have been nominated for the Booker-McConnell prize for fiction.

The wall of the shelter has been decorated with a multi-colour Q.P.R. KILL ARSENAL motif, the work of a local artist.

There'll be another one along soon.

SHOPPING TROLLEYS:

The New Look
For Old Bags

by Melvyn Bagg

The Tartan Shopping Trolley, that indispensable accessory for the dedicated bus-traveller 'just nipping down to the end of the road' has come a long way since it burst onto the scene in

Mrs Meg Potter gets caught shoplifting from Crufts.

1947. But then it will probably keep going for a while longer with perhaps a new pair of wheels and a replacement bag. Plus another handle.

But if you are buying new today you may be surprised at the choices available to the discerning 'wheeler-dealer'. Of course, there is the traditional *Royal Stuart* trolley. The stirring red and black check of the Stuart clan has long been associated with the Royal Family in Scotland and with the determined barker of shins, on and off buses, all over the country.

But now there are some alternatives to this familiar friend: for example, the all-weather version in McCaschill tartan. Very bright and breezy, if a little over the top. Or there's the 100% waterproof in MacKintosh. For the truly sporty there is the *Trolley Roadster*, finished in McAdam. Also very popular is the McDonald, though many find it utterly tasteless. An exciting Italian import is the impressive Macaroni. It can be a bit heavy, but it is great with onions and tomato.

Utterly British is the *Boadicea*. Comes in Woad Blue, Blood Red or Hemlock Green. Its main features are the blades, made in Sheffield steel by Stanley, which are attached to the wheels. Highly dangerous, of course, but very, very stylish. And just watch those school children, commuters and other riff-raff jump out of your way as you push your way down the aisle of a crowded No. 15!

Local Bus News
From London Buses

ROUTE 172 TO BRENT CROSS SHOPPING CENTRE FROM 28th MARCH

We're extending Monday to Friday Route 172 beyond Willesden Garage, Dudden Hill Lane, Neasden Underpass and Brent Cross to Dover, Calais, Brindisi, Ankara, Baghdad and Kabul. This will give a useful direct link for shoppers from mainland Turkey, the Northern Iraq marshes, West Afghanistan and the Pansher Valley. Buses will run between Brent Cross (John Lewis entrance) and Kabul every 20 minutes during the day and half-hourly in the evenings. There will be no service on Bank Holidays.

ROUTE 48A – STOP PRESS

We regret that new route 48A from Tesco Superstore, North Circular Road, via Brondesbury Road to Dover, Marseilles, Algiers and Tamanrasset, which has been operating on an experimental basis for passengers in the Tanezrouft, the Hoggar Mountains and other parts of the Central Sahara, has been withdrawn owing to lack of demand.

London Transport's replacement for the Routemaster.

Day 43

'It is cold. I mean cold. I thought the baths at school were chilly, but this is brisk. I can't even describe how cold it is. It certainly is cold, though. Absolutely freezing. Well, obviously. This is the North Pole, after all. All around me it's frozen. Snow to the left and to the right. And behind me for miles and miles and in front of me too, for miles and miles, now I come to mention it. So, you probably get the idea of what I am walking through: this big flat empty expanse of snow. Snow, snow, snow. Or perhaps ice, depending on how you choose to describe it. Probably snowy is best,

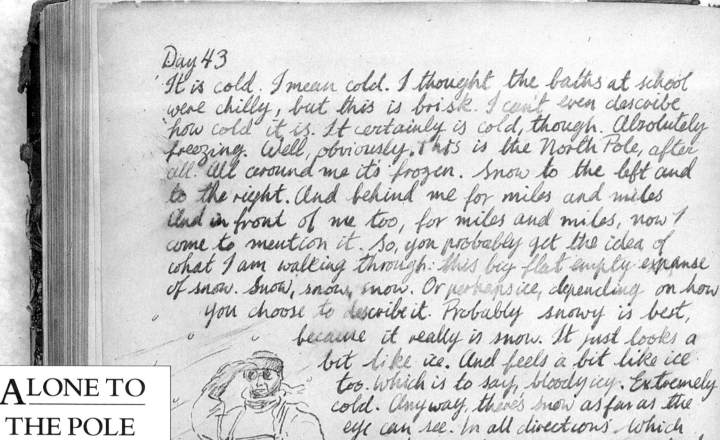

because it really is snow. It just looks a bit like ice. And feels a bit like ice too. Which is to say, bloody icy. Extremely cold. Anyway, there's snow as far as the eye can see. In all directions. Which is as far as the eye can see, in fact. Everywhere you look is snow. Exactly the same. Unchanging. Featureless. White and snow-like and, of course rather cold

Day 44

Its snowing again today. I am still alone. Alone with the snow. Its very strange, this place: strange and yet strangely familiar. This trip to the North Pole is just like my trip to the South Pole a few years ago. It was snowy then too. No, hang on. Is this the trip to the South Pole? Wasn't it the North Pole last time? What the hell, its bloody freezing anyway.

Day 45

Well, it's not got any warmer. It seems about as cold as yesterday. If not colder. But probably not very different. In fact, I should imagine that it is just about equally as cold as it was yesterday, certainly not any warmer anyway. The one thing you do notice, down here at the North Pole, is how cold it is. That and the snow, of course. In front of me today, for example,

ALONE TO THE POLE

THE DIARY OF SIR RANULPH TWISTLETON THINGE'S SOLO TREK TO THE POLE

the way I am walking, there is lots of snow. It is flat and lying in a flat sort of way sort of on top of itself, if you see what I mean. Exactly like it was yesterday. But that's hardly surprising because it is the same snow. Same sort of snow anyway. Snow which is white, flat & of course cold. And certainly not sand, or earth, or a motorbike, or anything like that. It is just snow. White snow. Snow which is somehow as white and cold as you might expect snow to be. Cold and white. White and cold. That just about sums it up. Behind me, of course it is entirely different. There is a huge bit of white flat, icy, cold snow, just like the bit in front, except that it has a dirty great line of footprints running through it. They're probably mine. Yes, almost definately mine, I should think. That would be right, wouldn't it? They look as if they could be mine. That's right, they come right up to my feet. My footsteps then, across the great wide expanse of white and cold snow. They could hardly be anybody else's, could they? Nobody would be mad enough to come down here in this weather.

It's much too cold.

Day 46
More snow... Do you know, there are 15 words in Eskimo for snow? And 33 for boredom?

Day 47
Cold again. And snowy. I must have a holiday when I get back from this. The Sahara Desert sounds appealing. All that heat. No snow. Just sand, sand and more sand. Noone but yourself for company for days on end — Or someone told me Benidorm is nice. Still only another 63 days to go and the Pole will be mine. I wonder how I'll recognise it, though. I hope there is some sort of stick or something. It would be nice to look at something other than all this snow. There's certainly a lot of it. All around. White and crisp and even.

I HATE WINDSURFERS

●

I hate windsurfers,
What a stupid lot they are,
With their stupid lumps of fibreglass
Stuck on their stupid car.

I hate windsurfers,
They do it standing up,
They could do it sitting in a ten-foot hole,
They'd still be stupid.

I hate windsurfers
In a totally irrational way,
It's probably something to do with their wet-suits,
Or maybe not, I can't say . . .

I hate windsurfers,
They're the sort that get me down.
I hope they fall in their reservoirs,
And swim a bit then drown.

I hate windsurfers,
La la la la,
I hate waterskiers as well,
Dah dee dah dah dah.

Thank you.

Ask Mel

For help with your personal financial problems write to Mel Cockney, former Motor Parts Dealer, now Senior City Analyst with stockbrokers De Kuyper, Nettlefold & Cockney, one time financial adviser to Guinness plc, Johnson Matthey Bankers and Keith Best.

. . . .

Dear Mel,
What is the best way to get into the City?

J.K., CHELMSFORD

In your case, down the A12, my son.

. . . .

Dear Mel,
What is the most tax efficient way to buy a run-down warehouse and convert it into luxury flats? Is it to allocate myself the most luxurious apartment and declare it to be my principal private residence and then distribute the building costs in a way that disguises my true capital gain?

G.R.J, SUFFOLK

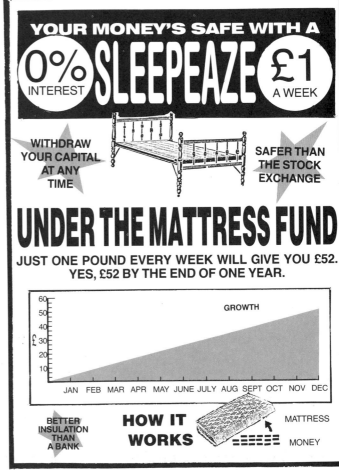

No, the most tax efficient way is not to tell the tax man about it.

. . . .

Dear Mel,

My accountant put me on to a great way of avoiding tax by covering huge areas of the Scottish Highlands with fast-growing conifers. The cost was limited to an initial start-up investment plus the total destruction of the local environment. But the last budget has apparently put paid to the tax advantages. Can you recommend a suitable tax avoidance scheme for, say, a TV personality on £500,000 a year?

T.W., SHEPHERD'S BUSH

Yes, it's a shame about the Chancellor knocking the forest scheme on the head. Selling heroin to teenagers is also restricted by bureaucratic red tape – otherwise a nice little earner well worth thinking about. Tell you what, you can get fantastic grants to start factories in areas of high unemployment and tax deals and everything. But it probably requires a bit of thought and some hard work. Not in your line of country if you're a TV personality, eh? I don't suppose you've thought about just paying your 40% tax and enjoying the rest of it without worrying about it?

. . . .

Dear Mel,
How do you become a name at Lloyds?
J.L. BATTERSEA

Search me. Probably change your name to Lloyd.

Dear Mel
Do you think it is worthwhile the small investor putting money into the stock market?
P.F. LONDON

The stock market these days is just a lottery. You might just as well back horses. Try Charlie's Angel in the 3 o'clock at Haydock Park.

. . . .

Dear Mel
What exactly is the futures market?
P.B.J., LIVERPOOL

It's what will happen in the stock exchange tomorrow.

. . . .

Dear Mel
I have recently inherited about £20,000 from my father's estate. Where would you say I should put it with a view to steady capital growth but where it can be available at shortish notice in case of emergency? I am 52 and have a wife but no children.
T.C.P., CROYDON

£20,000! Don't mess me about. Strewth, I had that sort of money in my back pocket when I was knocking out the dodgy motors. These days I spend that in lunches. Look, £20,000 is nothing. Do you know what I make in the City? Why don't you shove it in the Post Office if you're that worried? Otherwise get yourself a new car or have a bit of fun with a couple of tarts. You could piss it away in a couple of nights. There's nothing clever you can try with that sort of petty cash on the money markets, believe you me.

DOLLAR HAS BAD DAY IN NEW YORK

News of America's budget deficit hit the Dollar at the beginning of the day's trading. The currency, which has been weak for some months now, slumped back to bed and said it wouldn't get up again until it had had a little nap and a couple of aspirin.

By lunchtime, its long-term prospects looked better but the Dollar only felt up to a walk to the shops to get a paper and a packet of cigarettes. It said it was feeling distinctly light-headed and un-steady on its pins. Also, it had a bit of a gippy tummy and a nasty taste in its mouth.

By the close, the Dollar collapsed completely and had to be given cups of sweet tea followed by a nip of brandy. It didn't feel up to solids but thought it might try a soft boiled egg later on.

The Dollar then cancelled its engagements for the evening and went to bed early with a good book.

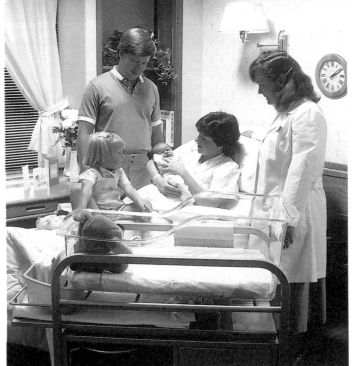

BUMFA
Your guide to private medicine

Health. It's one thing that frightens the willies out of you. Think of your darling wife. Think of your little kiddies. Think of them dying horribly.

Now give us your money.

BAND 1	Hip replacement Replacement of the hip Hippus bonus replacus The replacement of the bone in the top bit of your leg
BAND 2	Streptocemia Myxamatosis Disaphasis of the Peculum Renal Cortina Neuro Magnolia Wogan's Disease Urinary Coloctomy
BAND 3	The Harley Street Clinic, Whipps Cross The Harley St. Hospital, Luton The Harley St. Centre, Dagenham The Wigmore Consulting Cupboard, Harley St
BAND 4	Up to £5,000 Less than £10,000 All the anaesthetist's costs All the anaesthetist's fees All the anaesthetist's holidays The surgeon's fees up to £54,000

What sort of Health Care Plan are you looking for?

The choice is entirely yours.

Look carefully at these separate bands and decide what sort of cover you need.

Simply choose the band you require plus two or more from one band, but not from the other. If you choose the option marked ● then the other three bands may not apply, unless two or more bands have been selected twice.

We will make up an appropriate charge.

THE FACTS

● Here at BUMFA we have 5,000 trained nurses, doctors and consultants and 150,000 trained lawyers and insurance adjusters standing by in any emergency to scrutinize your claims.

● Our doctors and medical experts have all been trained in the greatest medical system in the world: the National Health Service of Great Britain.

DO NOT READ THIS BIT UNTIL YOU ARE ILL

Heart disease
Head disease
Leg disease
Foot or mouth disease
Diseases of the chest
Finger disease
Diseases of your inner bits
Disabilities, illnesses, or injuries of any kind are not covered by this policy.

BANKER'S ORDER. If you choose to pay by banker's order then we can keep upping our charges year by year and you won't even notice it happening.

APPLICATION FORM   Mr☐ Mrs☐ Miss☐ Ms☐

Initials └┴┴┘ Surname └┴┴┴┴┴┴┴┴┴┴┴┴┴┴┴┘
Address └┴┴┴┴┴┴┴┴┴┴┴┴┴┴┴┴┴┴┴┘
└┴┴┴┴┴┴┴┴┴┴┴┴┴┴┴┴┴┴┴┘
Please be sure to give
Postcode └┴┴┴┴┴┘
Telephone (home) └┴┴┴┴┴┴┴┴┴┴┴┴┴┘
(work) └┴┴┴┴┴┴┴┴┴┴┴┴┘

BLOCK CAPITALS PLEASE

I solemnly declare that I have never visited a doctor for any reason other than to get him to pay his green fees at the golf course. I don't even know what a doctor looks like. In fact, I have never felt better in my life. Tip top! Fighting fit! And even if I'm not, it's nothing to do with you lot at BUMFA anyway. I won't bother you unless · something really nasty crops up, or I fancy replacing my hip. So help me God.

FOR OFFICE USE ONLY		
DATE RECEIVED		
SERIAL NO		
STUPID	YES	NO
RICH	YES	NO
ILL	YES	NO
MAD	YES	NO
GULLIBLE	YES	NO

SMALL PRINT. If you are having trouble with your eyes, then we refuse utterly to take responsibility for them.

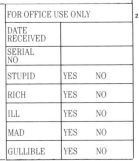

1. Dr Harley J. Street. (Our Founder.)

2. BUMFA was responsible for the building of this fully equipped modern bank in Geneva.

3. Enjoy the sociable atmosphere of the private VD Clinic.

4. A patient enjoys a light post operative breakfast with his surgeon.

BUMFA

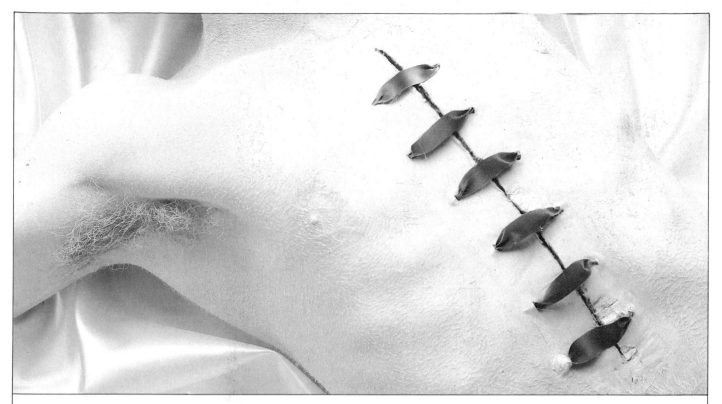

H.M. Government WARNING:
SMOKING CAN CAUSE YOU TO HAVE ONE OF
YOUR LUNGS REMOVED

20
YEARS *of*
BRITISH
ROAD MARKINGS

FIRST DAY COMMEMORATIVE ISSUE

'OH, SUCH WONDROUS GAGS'

THE TOMB OF MANNY ISAACS, ONE-LINER WRITER TO KING TUT, UNCOVERED IN THE VALLEY OF THE KINGS

FRANKIE HOWERD'S ACT ON PYRAMID WALLS

SOME of the world's oldest jokes saw the light of day for the first time in a thousand years, here today. They were found, as originally written, in hieroglyphics on the wall, before being 'rewritten' by King Tut, Egypt's top comic and Pharaoh, for his cabaret act.

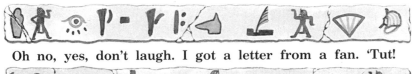

Oh no, yes, don't laugh. I got a letter from a fan. 'Tut!

I think you're fantastic. Please excuse the crayon,

but they don't allow sharp instruments in here.'

Producer of the brilliantly rubber *Spitting Image*, Professor John Lloyd, a world-famous authority on what is funny, said, 'We are delighted by the find. We thought we'd put every old joke there was on the screen, but this definitely means another series.'

But already there is some dispute over who owns the gags. Egypt has refused the material an export licence. 'Ever since Ramses II's "leaky oboe" gag turned up in Billy Connolly's stage show we have been on the track of the gag-robbers. Some of these jokes are over two thousand years old. They should be left to die in peace.'

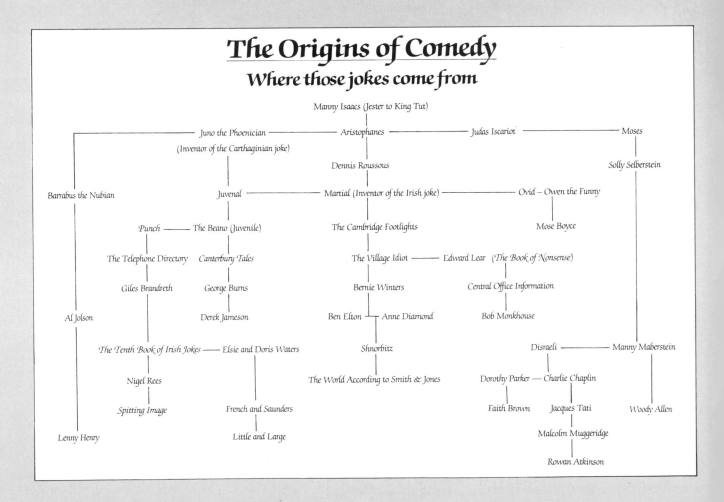

The Origins of Comedy
Where those jokes come from

IF YOU LIVED IN A SHITHOLE LIKE THIS YOU WOULDN'T GIVE A XXXX WHAT YOU DRANK EITHER.

A POSTCARD FROM BELGIUM

Le Slammer De Bruxelles en Printemps.

God what a shite hole.
Still you're used to it.
Here isn't much beter
neether. Time is pasing
slow, like watching Arsenal.
I don't know what the weather
is like. We've been playing
football with the warders.
Bloody boring game it
is too. Please send us
the rules.
Your loving son
Jimmy

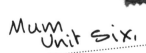

Mum
Unit Six,
Eric Heffer House

Cilla Buildings,

Liverpool,

England.

PRINTED
IN
E.E.C

100/329

OTHER PEOPLE'S SUNDAY LUNCH

213: PETER LANGAN

Survey report: 13 Hazelcroft Road, London NW6 (Contd.)

..in the near future. No tests were applied to any of the services (hot and cold water supplies, gas and electrical installations) and you may wish to have independent tests carried out in order to satisfy yourself as to what defects, if any, exist.

The soil drainage and surface water systems are possibly combined and enter a single public sewer, but as the systems are generally inaccessible we are not able to comment upon the precise nature of the drainage arrangements. It is possible that the various drains are connected to a common drain laid at the rear of this and adjoining properties but we were not able to ascertain whether or not this is the case. Similarly it is not possible to comment upon the condition of the underground conduits without applying a proper test and, in the absence of suitable access points, such a test would be impossible to carry out - or indeed possible, as the case may be.

It is reasonable to assume that the main roof is probably in a generally satisfactory condition; if it is not, then something should be done about it.

As to the internal structure of the roofing and its member parts, this we would also safely take to be in either a generally satisfactory or unsound condition.

With regard to the general state of repair of the main lounge, the kitchen, the hallway, the staircase, the landing, the main bedroom, the two single bedrooms and the bathroom, we must confine our opinions to

Survey report: 13 Hazelcroft Road, London NW6 (Contd.)

observations consistent with the fact that, due to a lack of suitable parking space in the area at the time and the pressures of a particularly crowded schedule for us that afternoon, our only visual access to the property was by means of binoculars from our car travelling down Westway Flyover at sixty-five miles an hour. We therefore conclude that the above property is in all probability either detached, semi-detached, possibly terraced, of contemporary, Victorian,Edwardian, Georgian, Tudor or some other architectural period in style, with main walls and brickwork requiring either a)a certain amount of repair b)none at all, with 60' rear garden - larger or smaller dimensions not to be discounted - and whose general structural condition is comparable to any similar building of its age with or without serious defects, and that the asking price is a reasonable reflection of current market value.

Yours faithfully,

Mo. K. Mah

Our fees: £970.00
+ VAT

PS. If it does not reflect current market value, then do not touch it with a bargepole. (Unless you're really keen on it - in which case, go for it.)

The Complete Works of William Shakespeare

 His brain

 His Liver

His Left Lung (seen from front)

His Right Lung (seen from back)

His foot

To be or not to be
Another one of his feet

 His Ileum

His colon

 His semi colon

His small intestine

His Large intestine

His bloody huge intestine

 Shakespeare's kidney

 His kidney bean

 His bean

 Has been

His pet dog

His pet fish

 His pet hate

 His quill

His quill supplier

 His willy

 His bollocks (COMEDY of ERRORS)

 His tights

 The shrew that inspired "The Taming of the Shrew"

 The inspiration for the first part of "King Henry VI"

 The second part

 The third part

 His Anachronism

Personal microprocessor Shakespeare was perfecting when he gave up electronics to become a playwright

A plug for Shakespeare's microprocessor

 MACBETH IS BRILLIANT CATCH IT IF YOU CAN!
A plug for Shakespeare's play

 The other end of his bloody huge intestine

An example of blank verse

DESIGNER
THINGS

1 **CLUBBING?**
In Paris they're wearing
the latest thing in London.
Waxed Cotton Swimming Trunks.
And Uniroyal Hunter Flippers.
Both from Saliva of Soho.

2 **JAPANESE HI TECH**
Authentic salt miner's
hard hat.
With clip-on light.
Never lose your contact lenses
in the Limelight again.
£16.50. Branches of Dorothy
Perkins.

3 **CARRY CLASSIC**
Co-Op plastic bags.
In light-duty plastic with
the Co-Op logo on one side only.
Based on the original 1974
design by Garry Tompsett.
Available from Fiorucci for £8.50.
Or free from branches of the
Co-Op with purchases above 20p.

4 **ALABAMA CLASSIC**
WONDERS
Original United States Welfare
Issue, for the Sightless Black.
As worn by Rev Gary Davies,
'Little' Stevie Wonder etc.
Cutler and Gross.
Price on application.

5 **WET, WET, WET**
Brazilian industrial
galoshes.
In flaky blue asbestos.
£4. Mail order only.

6 BEACH BUM
The Giorgio Armani
Birthday Suit.
The Designer label for the
nudist beach.
Complete with tube of yellow
rubber adhesive.
£700. Armani outlets.

7 DESIGN CLASSIC
The original 'Nut and
Bolt'.
In high carbon tempered steel.
By Guest, Keen and Nettleford of
Iron Bridge.
Available from Ironmongers,
Jasper Conran's new accessories
shop in Beauchamp Place.

8 SERIOUS GRAFFITI
East German Paint-
Shop Kit.
Up to twenty trains a night.
Choice of colours.
Available by mail order.
Wehrmachtsurpluszupplei.
Lenin Strasse. Lubeck. DDR.

**9 SONY REMOTE-
CONTROL CONTROL**
Remote control find.
Bleeps once when you enter
the room.
Never lose your remote
control again.
All good electrical shops.

10 PUSSY GALORE
New York designer cat
litter.
Grey plastic tray filled
with five thousand industrial
ball bearings.
Wash and re-use.
Available from Dalmation.
The original black and white
pet supply store.

11 B. WATCH
No disfiguring hands,
no clumsy numbers.
In pure black.
Timeless elegance from
Yoshi Yoshitomato.

M & G

THE ENCYCLOPAEDIA TEENAGEIA

– the indispensable manual for all Channel 4 Commissioning Editors, Janet Street-Porter, and alternative comedians

AMERICA – Basically, the United States of America is corrupt, reactionary and economically imperialist, though it does have great rock music and jeans. Its power and influence is definitely on the wane: baseball shirts have not been smart for weeks. The last great President of America was John F. Kennedy who was shot in Dallas (unless that was J.R. Ewing). Presidents since Kennedy have been rich and corrupt and have lacked his great vision and teeth. Also note: Greyhound bus tickets round America are cheaper if you book from England.

EDUCATION – Exams should be abolished. Some people are good at learning up stuff for exams and others aren't. Some of the cleverest people in the world failed exams, Einstein for example. Isaac Newton probably. Everybody should be entitled to as much education as they want. People should be judged on their true merit, not on paper qualifications. School uniforms should be abolished and everyone allowed to express their individuality by going to school in jeans and trainers.

CONSPIRACIES – It is a well-known fact that a way of running cars on water was invented years ago but the patents were all bought up by the oil companies or General Motors so the idea could be kept a secret to protect their profits.

LAW AND ORDER – The Police only arrest the wrong people and beat confessions out of them. You only have to read one of those books on Christie or Dr Crippen. Also Jack the Ripper was probably innocent. Judges are all old men who are out of touch with real people.

RELIGION – Children should not be brought up in any particular religion. Everyone should be taught about Christianity, Mohammedanism, Buddhism, Shinty and all world religions, and then left to make their own minds up to become atheists.
God can't exist, otherwise he wouldn't let earthquakes happen.

THE BOMB – Nuclear weapons are bad. Nuclear power is bad. Nuclear families are bad.

BEN ELTON – Great comedian until he sold out to LWT.

LITERATURE – Shakespeare is over-rated. So is Dickens. Anyway, it's pointless dissecting novels anyway; you should just read them. The best writers ever are J.R.R. Tolkien and Douglas Adams.

LATIN AND GREEK – Should not be taught in schools because they are dead languages and also very hard to learn. Anyway, English is well known to be the *lingua franca* of the modern world. It would be much better to learn Russian or Japanese except they are even more difficult.

SOCIETY – The world would be a much better place if it was run by young people and not old people who have sold out. For example, Richard Branson. People are the same the world over, it's the system and politicians that are to blame.

THIRD WORLD – Starvation in the Third World is caused by the high interest rates charged on loans by banks and low prices paid for things like cocoa that Third World countries produce. Everyone in the world (who, as a matter of fact, could all fit on the Isle of Wight if they stood close together) could have enough food to eat overnight if only they would listen to Bob Geldof and the Common Market didn't have food mountains.

·· THE ··
ULTIMATE
TIME-SHARE
OPPORTUNITY

Thirty minutes with MEL SMITH in the restaurant of his choice

● Celebrity Interval Ownership are proud to present a premier opportunity in leisure investment facilities.

● Imagine! You and up to three of your family or friends could spend 30 minutes a year in the company of world-famous funny man, Mel Smith, each and every year for the rest of time*.

● Or you could swap your 30 minutes with Mel Smith for 30 minutes with another celebrity of equal stature, anywhere in the world: Pete Murray; Ray Allan and 'Lord Charles' (two for the price of one); Lars Benjison, Norway's Top Magic Man.
A world of choice is yours.

MELVYN KENNETH SMITH IS YOURS
● Fully furbished.
● Maid service.
● Sleeps four.
● British owned and managed.
● Guaranteed at least 3 grunts of acknowledgement.

● Will call you by name. (Not necessarily your own.)
● Complete insurance arranged.

Don't be left out in the lobby! Reserve your place in the *Sun* with the ultimate status symbol.

INSPECTION

Come down to our special no-obligation Open Day to get shown around Mel Smith, and you will automatically qualify for a free month with Griff Rhys Jones.

*Or until he dies, whichever is the sooner.

EXIT TOURS

THE ULTIMATE ADVENTURE HOLIDAYS

EXCITEMENT AND ACTION
or
YOUR PASSPORT BACK

OUR GUARANTEE
We haven't got one, but it looks exciting, doesn't it?

*Breakfast
in Beirut.*

*The quickest
way home.*

*The '89 Itinerary for the
Outwardly Bound.*

DAY ONE.
Pick-up by a Greek-owned
ten-year-old mini cab driven
by an Italian. Trip round
Foggy London Town's M25
in the legendary morning
'rush-hour'.
Rendezvous with microlight
jet revving up on the dockside
runway at the City Airport.
Bottom-deck berth on the
Spirit of Free Parking,
flagship of the Liberian Cross
Channel Ferry Service.
Channel crossing under the command of ex-bosun,
and former Torrey Canyon Look-Out, Admiral
Dimitri Onassis.

DAY TWO.
Minibus picks up you, and your seventeen
travelling companions, from a central reservation
on the Périphérique.
High-speed dash on the French motorway system
on the first day of the French national holidays.
Breakfast at L'Auberge de Grand Vin.
Lunch at Restaurant de Cognac et Schnapps.
Dinner at the Tango Mango Brandy Bar.
Night drive through the French Alps with eighty-
four-year-old *maître* Jacques Boozier at the wheel.

DAY THREE.
Breakfast in Austrian ski resort of Klonkers.
Off-piste powder-skiing across the North Face of
'L'Avalanche', graveyard of the brave.
Display of skeet shooting beneath 'Old Crackly', the
largest glacial overhang in Austria.
High-speed Sikorski double-rotor helicopter
mountain-hop to southern Italy's bandit country.
Evening free for solo exploration of the old
'Comorra' Quarter.

DAY FOUR.
Dip in the waters of the Bay of Naples, last breeding
ground of some of the most endangered species of
streptococci in the world.
Issue of stomach pumps and new American
passports.
El Al flight for breakfast in Beirut.
Tour of the mosques of mainly Christian West
Beirut with a guide from the CIA University of
Baghdad.

DAY FIVE.
Assemble Kuwait Oil Terminal Three.

Board unflagged, unescorted supertanker for cruise
through the Gulf of Arabia.

DAY SIX.
Cruise Gulf.
(If time.) View Islamic Fundamentalist gun boats.
Mine spotting. (Subject to aerial bombing.)

DAY SEVEN.
Bed and board in a bisexual brothel, Mombassa.
Flight by reconditioned DC 10 to join Sri Lanka's
Independence Day Celebrations.
'Packed lunches' provided to carry through
Malaysian customs.
Riverboat cruise to view the Bangladeshi monsoon
season.
Shark fishing from a Phillipine
ferry during Typhoon Mori.
Excursion to explore the French-
occupied atolls of the South Seas
by rubber dinghy, courtesy of
Greenpeace. (Optional.)

DAY EIGHT.
Carnival at the Labour Day Anti-
American Demonstration in
Santiago.
Guided tour of the dungeons of
the Charity School with Captain
'Three' Pinochet.
Lunch at the hospital of your
choice, in Panama City.
Board one-engined converted
fighter, provided by Contra Carriers for your low-
level flight across Nicaraguan airspace and on to the
USA border. (Your only companions are the
coughing of the engine, the remoteness of the
Mexican jungle and the seventy-two-pound bag of
handmilled cocaine nestling between your legs.)

DAY NINE.
Tour of Pittsburgh Industrial Areas by open car.
Walk: historic Harlem by night.

DAY TEN.
Early start, because the first zephyrs of an
unforecast hurricane are waiting to waft your giant
inflated condom-shaped balloon, Virgin Shroud, up
into the stormy skies above the North Atlantic.

DAY ELEVEN.
Unscheduled touch-down in the middle of a
traditional IRA funeral in the historic Falls Road
area of old Belfast. (Small arms provided.)

Return home, in a souvenir body bag from Macey's
of old New York.

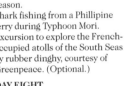

*Off piste
powder skiing on
L'Avalanche.*

*Cruise on
the Gulf.*

*Dip in the
waters of the
Bay of Naples.*

EXIT TOURS

*WE MAKE THE
GOING EASY.*

THE ELIZABETH TAYLOR STORY

YES the fabulous, larger than cliché story of one of the world's most famous screen goddesses of all time ... Elizabeth Taylor

ELIZABETH TAYLOR – THE ACTRESS

Just to mention Elizabeth Taylor's name (Elizabeth Taylor) conjures up her many commanding performances in such classic motion pictures as ... er, well now ... what has she been in recently? Or ever, come to that?

Ah yes, some of the notable films of Elizabeth Taylor's career were, of course ... *International Velvet, Lassie*

brought Elizabeth Taylor most notoriety and diamonds. Son of a Welsh pit pony, Richard Burton's performance as Hamlet, Prince of Denmark astonished the critics in 1947, coming as it did in an Oxford student production of *King Lear*. He was tipped for the very top. Kenneth Tynan saw him as the Roger Moore of his generation. But addiction to drink, marrying Elizabeth Taylor and appearing in bad movies ruined an otherwise unmemorable career.

▲ Poor old cow

It's often said that a beautiful woman would look good even in a sack, but not Liz Taylor. Mind you, television looks good ▶

What strange allure does this Goddess have for the menfolk of the world? ▼

ELIZABETH TAYLOR – THE WIT

Elizabeth Taylor's witty ripostes are legendary (i.e. mostly made up). Typical is her famous exchange with Princess Margaret:

Princess Margaret	Have you come far?
Elizabeth Taylor	Quite a way, considering my ability. How about you?
Princess Margaret	And what is it you do?
Elizabeth Taylor	Have you got a diamond as big as this?
Princess Margaret	I must just go and open something.
Elizabeth Taylor	Me too.
Both	Who was that fat old cow?

Come Home, Lassie Goes to RADA, Lassie on Heat, Lassie's Getting Fat, Carry On Cleo, National Velvet's Animal House, Who's Afraid of Virginia Slims, Gone With the Burton, A Diamond As Big as Her Tits and many, many more. And some even, even worse.

ALEXANDER WALKER writes, '... To be with Elizabeth Taylor is to be in the presence of a great star. Well, at least, it was when she was married to Richard Burton.'

ELIZABETH TAYLOR – THE WOMAN

Elizabeth Taylor's private life has, if anything, been more glamorous than her performances on screen. It has certainly been better acted. She has married eight husbands to date. They include:

- Arthur Miller
- Roger Vadim
- Richard Burton Part I
- Montague Burton
- Richard Burton Part II
- Sir Ralph Halpern
- Richard Burton, the early years
- Henry VIII

But it was her marriage and re-marriage to Richard Burton which

ELIZABETH TAYLOR – THE STAR

The on- and off-screen career of Miss Taylor will be examined in minutest detail (e.g. her talent). Just what is it that links such screen immortals as Elizabeth Taylor, Zsa Zsa Gabor, Sabrina and Joan Collins? Is it just that there is always one of them on Aspel & Co? Or is there more to it than that?

Dressed up as a corkscrew to appeal to Richard Burton
▼

◀ Richard Burton in the original Off-Broadway production of *When Did You Last See My Trousers!*

Find out in
THE ELIZABETH TAYLOR STORY

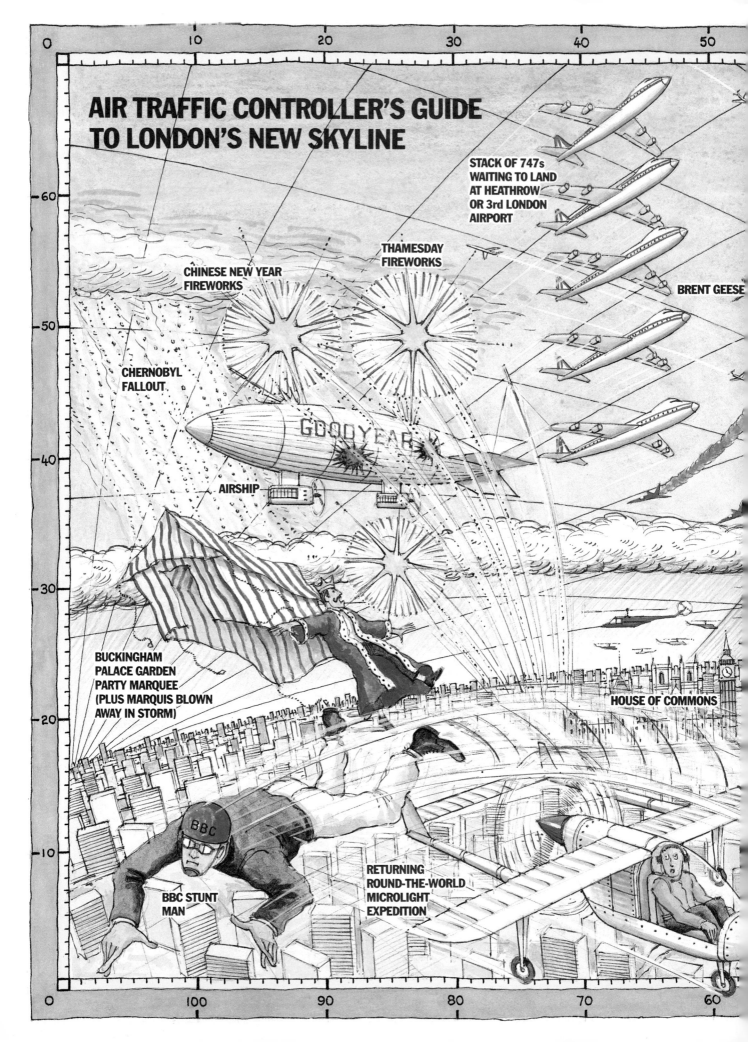

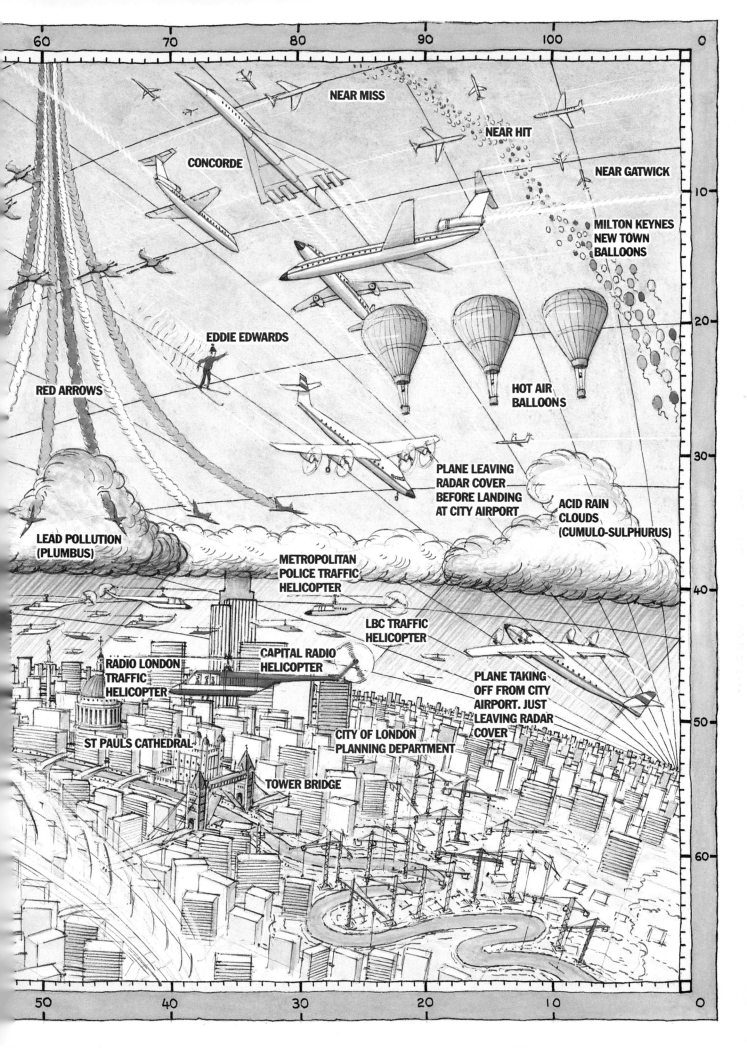

When you've had a few and you're miles from home, it's not your brain that does the thinking.

These words were spoken by Michael. He is the controller of a large television channel. Four years ago he started showing documentaries and dramas about AIDS; people who have AIDS; people who might have AIDS and don't know about it; people who might not have AIDS and don't know about it; people who might not have AIDS but do know about it; people who might not have AIDS, might not know about it, and don't want to know about it, and immunologists.

He has never had a homosexual experience, nor has he taken drugs.

To protect him, his name and some of the details have been changed, but in all other respects the story is true.

'You could say I'm part of the generation that thinks it invented television. I'm not saying that all programme controllers behave like I do. Some people in Grampian still think AIDS is a potential advertising account for fat ABC 1 women... But most of them do, and they're going to bore everybody to death if they carry on.'

TEMPTATIONS

'When you're in charge of a whole television channel and you've come to the end of a really tough week putting all those different television programmes into different times in an evening, you feel you deserve something more exciting than *Twenty-One Years of the Two Ronnies.*

'Perhaps I'd be with a few colleagues down the club. I'd have had a few. Somebody would suggest, half jokingly, that we could have a bit of fun if we could get sex and death rolled into one.

'Or I'd be at lunch, and they'd sit me next to some pretty slip of a drama producer. She'd whisper in my ear. Maybe suggest a little bit of late-night harrowing.

'It all seemed so simple.

'Of course, I never even thought about condoms.

'Then, suddenly, I found I was thinking of nothing else.

'Up to then, the biggest danger that a bit of casual sex represented was a cup of tea with Mary Whitehouse.

'But everything changed.'

CONSEQUENCES

'In 1980 I ran an AIDS Special on BBC2.

'After that, there was no more trouble until several months later.

'Just after the *News*, I stuck in what I thought was a harmless Gritty Drama. You know the sort of thing. Businessman has it away with tart, gets deadly killer virus, gives wife excellent acting opportunity, looks thin, dies.

'It was just a bit of fun.

'But I still thought an AIDS documentary was something that happened to other people.

'Then one day my brain went numb. I realised I had put out an Esther Rantzen Probe, a Charity Benefit for The Terrence Higgins Trust and an In-Depth Look at a Man with Shaved Head Being Cheerful in the same evening.

'It was a terrible shock. I went to see my DG. I was diagnosed AIDS positive. The knowledge almost destroyed me completely. There was absolutely nothing I could do. My brain went even more numb.

'Before I knew it, I had Alternative Comedians sticking rubber johnnies on their fingers during a Figure Skating Gala. I had four hours of Joan Bakewell and those eyebrows. I gave a Richard Branson Publicity Stunt free airtime on the British Broadcasting Corporation.

'When it comes down to it, it isn't difficult to die. What's difficult is watching someone else do it four nights a week.'

AVOIDING AIDS

Eventually, with help, Michael started a new life and eventually infected another channel. But since he left the BBC, the risk of death from watching AIDS programmes has become greater than ever.

You can avoid it only by taking sensible precautions. Never watch a television programme after nine o'clock at night. Never watch a television programme before nine o'clock at night. Never read a Sunday paper again. Always wear a condom stuffed in each ear. (Use only a clean condom or you may catch Deaf Aids.) Remember, if you watch one documentary about this terrible killer disease you are watching every documentary ever made about this killer disease. TV Producers are notoriously promiscuous with their ideas. Your life could depend on it.

SAFE SEX IT'S MORE FUN THAN **A**NOTHER **I**NTERMINABLE **D**OCUMENTARY **S**CREENING.

MEL SMITH'S PROBLEM PAGE

JOE ORTON

COMMEMORATIVE MATCHING DOILY & TABLECLOTH SET

THEY WERE LOVERS
BUT TALENT TORE THEM ASUNDER

Here is an offer no fan or collector of ORTONANIA can afford to be without.

It is nearly seventeen years since the horribly disfigured body of Joan Bakewell was discovered on *Late Night Line Up*. Now she reveals that she too had a nodding acquaintance with the great homosexual and playwright **JOE ORTON**.

JOAN BAKEWELL writes:

"Joe was always surrounded by lots of people called Kenneth. Apart from that I can't remember much about him, but what a lovely person he was etc. etc. blah and I'm sure he would find this tablecloth and doily very useful."

Everybody loved twinkly-eyed, huge-penised Joe.

Internationally acclaimed voice-over artist for frogs **KENNETH BENNET** writes:

"I have a lot in common with Joe. I am a writer. I come from oop North. I wear similar trousers. And, of course, I go to Tunisia for my holidays."

Who will ever forget his great plays: *A Prick up Your Arse, Loo, If I had a Hammer, Camping Around a Bit, Camping Around a Bit More.*

Kenneth Lahr is Joe's autobiographer and son of the legendary Lahr de Lahr, the cowardly comedian in the MGM's classic, *The Wizard of Oz*, and he also wrote a book about Joe Orton or something like that . . . Anyway, we couldn't get hold of him but that doesn't make much difference because nobody's quite sure who he is, let alone his father.

Guarantee If you are not entirely and absolutely satisfied with your purchase we **guarantee** that we will be out of business within twenty-five days, and unavailable for any refunds or discussion, even if you turn up with a BBC camera crew and a foot-in-the-door reporter.

Dear 'Ortonly Yours', Please rush me ☐ Joe Orton Commemorative Matching Doily and Tablecloth sets, PLUS, if I respond within ten days, my FREE copy of *Here I Sit, Broken-Hearted*. I enclose a postal order for a large sum of money.

Address: Cloth Scam, Ortonly Yours, Cottage Industries, Barking.

PEGGY (KENNETH) RAMSAY writes:

"This great work of fiction was considered lost until it was discovered on the walls of the Public Urinal in the Finchley Road, known as 'The Swiss Cottage', where Joe spent almost the whole of 1964.

A PEEP AT GENIUS.
Here is a sneak extract from the great masterpiece.

POLICEMAN (taking the knickers off his head): Balls! By Picasso.

SCOUTMASTER: Buy me and stop one.

POLICEMAN: Dislexia rlues K.O.

© Nigel Rees Industries

AUBERON LAHR writes:

"I usually plug the Folio Society, but this is rather similar although I am, of course, prejudiced against homosexuals in general and Joe Orton in particular, but this play is probably a work of genius, I should think. Be lucky!"

PAUNCH

YET ANOTHER
NUMBER

TREVOR DUNTON

CONTENTS

PAUNCH *Spring Number*

WILL THIS DO?

Stanley Matthew-Keating

'The staff and boys of the Njingo High School, Nyere, warmly applauded the Transport Minister's speech and at the end of his visit gave him three hearty chairs'

NAIROBI STAR AND REPORTER

Well, I must say, I've never been given three chairs. Let alone a trio of pieces of furniture you could in any way describe as hearty. What makes a chair hearty, anyway, I wonder. Were they once owned by Dr Christian Barnard? Or are they made out of the insides of artichokes? Or is the whole thing a misprint? Probably, but I can still use it to get going on my piece for this week. Mind you, it's a tiresome – and lonely – life being a writer. And especially so if you write for *Paunch,* the famous humourless magazine, because nobody ever reads anything you write after about the first line. Right, that must be the first paragraph done by now.

And the second.

And third.

FOURTH PARAGRAPH

The funny thing is that I actually read some of the articles in a copy of *Paunch* myself the other day. Not just my page-filler about the amusing things that occur to me when looking at a pile of old news clippings. No, I was going on a long train journey and I bought a copy of *Paunch* to read because I was too embarrassed to get a porn mag and I'd forgotten to bring a P.G. Wodehouse novel with me. I've got it in front of me as I write.

Now, I've often heard people say that the only good things in *Paunch* are the cartoons. But nothing could be further from the truth. For a start, there is a double-page spread of cartoons by MAHOOD which I would defy Mahood's own mother to laugh at if he was spraying her with Nitrous Oxide.

Here's another huge cartoon in full colour which doesn't appear to have a joke in it at all. It's by Jensen. It looks like – why do *Paunch* cartoonists make their signatures so difficult to read? Several other cartoons are fairly obviously rejects from the *New Yorker*. Of course, there's always David Langdon. I'm not sure why, but there he always is. Luckily for him he is in the middle of a page by Libby Purves so his drawing looks quite hysterical in comparison with her article. Is she writing a letter to her mother or being a journalist or what?

TAKE OUT A FEW WORDS TO USE AS SUB-HEADING FOR NEXT BIT

There's somebody called Robert Buchman doing a very clever bit this week. It's a cruel parody of the very worst of sixth-form or medical-school humour. It's absolutely crammed with silly semi-jokes about parts of the body... Hmm, God knows what Hunter Davis is writing about. I couldn't get through more than a few lines on the train without falling asleep, which was irritating as I was intending to knock together a few lines about the train journey in my usual droll way. You know the sort of thing: 'the man opposite me spent the whole journey looking through his papers and adding up figures on his calculator.' That's the trouble with your average Yuppie... Well, of course you know the sort of thing as I write something like that every other week. And so, it seems, does every other writer on the magazine.

Is that enough yet? No, no quite. Oh, twiddle plom plom qwertyuiopasd... well, that's another paragraph done.

WE'VE GOT TO BREAK UP THE ACRES OF TEXT SOMEHOW

Of course, we all had a bit of a fright when the old Editor left: Alan Coren... Is there anybody still reading this far? Don't worry, there'll be a whisky advert along soon or a cartoon by Heath if you're really lucky. That's if they still have his stuff in... Anyway, there was talk of a new broom, many changes, so I thought my days might be numbered. But it turned out they appointed the Assistant Editor in his place – his name escapes me at the moment – who churns out this sort of drivel himself, so I'm still here and so are Hunter and Sheridan and Russell and the rest.

And apparently if the worst comes to the worst and you are Roy Hattersley or Melvyn Bragg or someone like that you can get your stuff into the *Listener* now anyway. Oh well, that's it. Invoice follows.

*The man who laughed at Paunch.
With apologies to H.E. Bateman
(but none to Mr Paunch)*

airports, hydro electric dams, patios – we are the specialists

garden rockery, suspension bridges – ask the experts

STUBBS & SON

352 Cricklewood Broadway, NW2
452-3771 (1 line)

3 March

	£	s	d
Estimate 003: ½ To build ^ Channel Tunnel Labour and materials incl. to hack away entire continental Shelf Substratum connecting British Isles to European Mainland and remove in skip(s) as provided To replace shingle beach as before and make good To provide :– 13 mile Cable Extention lead – 11 mile x 250' RSJ Railway terminal – ~~French doors and Crazy paving~~ at entrance to tunnel (Damp Course extra)			
Total	£12,850,000,000		

10% Supplement if high tide →

please leave spare set of keys

Cash please

'MY WALES AND

Says Griffith Rhys Jones, well-known person of Welsh origins.

Unemployment in Wales has been halved by the recent job creation scheme ... This young girl is a traffic sign signaller.

Harry Secombe at the commercial opening of his latest chin.

Tom Jones popping in for a quick pint of Old Druids Poison at his local – The Las Vegas Hilton.

The Queen adjusts the Prince of Wales' ceremonial dalmation skin overcoat to hide his snooker-playing personal detective.

Cardiff's top eatery.

'HOW GREEN WAS MY TOURIST'

When I was a boy, I was lucky enough to be able to wander at will in the beautiful hills and valleys of my home town of Epping in North London. But some of the closest members of my family have always lived in Wales. Especially my mother and my father. And they kept getting the police to bring me back.

Today I remember my roots, especially the turnips and swedes which they eat instead of vegetables over there.

Nowadays, I am always being asked to go back to Wales, mainly by people in England, but sometimes for some special charity Welsh celebration in poetry and song.

Somehow I never seem to be able to go. I have to stay in my swimming pool in my converted warehouse in North London and practice my Cockney accent.

But, in my heart of hearts, I know that Cymru will always be there, the hills, and ... the hills, as old as time itself, and not half as boring. About a quarter though.

Today's visitor to Wales should not be surprised if he finds the locals all talking in the beautiful native tongue. It's only because he has just walked into the shop. If he wasn't there they'd be talking English just like anybody else.

WALES THE LAND WHERE HISTO

WELCOME TO IT,

Some other famous Welsh people:
Mavis Nicholson
Ruth Madoc.
Tom Jones (the singer).
Bob Dylan.

THE GREAT FESTIVALS OF WALES

The Eisteddfodd. (The Bards v the Druids at
Cardiff Arms Park. Every year on the 'telly'.)
The Welsh New Year. At which Welsh people
say: 'Well, that's another year over, then.'

WALES: LAND OF SONG AND SINGING
TALENT

Harry Secombe.
Dai Francis.
Grace Jones.
Andy Williams.
And lots of others too.

EXPERIENCE THE CRAFTS OF WALES

Hand-carved lumps of Coalite shaped into
comical Welsh pixies and leprechauns.
Wind-up Harry Secombes.
Knitting.

WHERE THE TABLE GROANS

Welsh food is famous throughout Wales. It is
what Welsh people love to eat. They prefer it
to coal. Delicious cold ham salad. Welsh
cakes. Welsh biscuits. Welsh sandwiches.
Welsh Heinz Tomato Ketchup and Seaweed,
which is called lava bread because it is
thrown up all over the mountains.

Some famous Welsh princes:

The Prince of Wales.
The Prince of Wales.
The Prince of Wales.
The Prince of Wales.

Famous Welsh drinks:

Nice cup of tea.
Half pint of beer. (Not Sundays.)
Scotch whisky.
Malibu, the Taste of the Tropics.

Welsh National Costume:

Shirt, look you.
Tie, look you.
Cardigan, see. (Named after famous place
in Wales.)

TEACH YOURSELF WELSH

Because nobody else will bother to.

Newcomers to Wales
receive instruction on how
to blend in with the nation
by putting traffic cones on
their heads.

Grace Jones – ecstatic after
signing her advertising
contract with Flymo Lawn
Mowers.

Andy Williams is awarded
'Best Dressed Man in
Wales'.

EEPS AND SO DOES EVERYBODY ELSE.

For those readers who prefer not to smoke the right-hand side of this page has been designated a non-smoking area.

RadioTomes

UPFRONT

BY NICKI HOUSEHOLD

In At The Deep End
Wednesday 9.30pm, BBC 1

'Sometimes White City can look just like Beirut on a wet Sunday afternoon,' muses Paul Heiney as he sips coffee, staring out of the window of his office at TV Centre, Wood Lane. And he should know . . . He's just come back from the Middle East, filming for a new series of his ever-popular programme.

This time he had been given a week to train as a double agent for Israeli intelligence. I asked him if the experience had been frightening. 'In a word – yes,' he says, reaching for another digestive biscuit. 'The situation's so volatile out there. Just put one foot out of line, keep mixing Egypt up with Israel

or something like that and they really take umbrage. One night, coming into the Gaza Strip, I told the taxi driver that I was beginning to think this whole East Bank–West Bank business was a bit of a song and dance about nothing and I really couldn't understand what all the fuss was about. You know what happened? He got really huffy.'

Had this been one of his hardest assignments? Pause for thought. He sips his coffee and takes another biscuit. 'Last month in that air-traffic-control centre at Heathrow took some beating. Not only were all those pilots so impatient to land but they always wanted a whole runway to themselves at a time. But as the day went on, I picked up some very useful ideas – fog and 747s definitely don't mix; it really does pay to concentrate all the time; and catnapping is a no-no. It's not fair on the passengers, otherwise.'

Is the routine getting too demanding? Are he and Chris Searle being asked to achieve too much in too short a time? 'Let's face it, it wouldn't be the same if there

wasn't an element of challenge about it all.'

'I agree,' a voice booms. Enter Chris Searle looking flushed and a little the worse for wear. Yes, it had been a long session in the BBC Bar, but could anyone blame him? Spending all morning at a medical tribunal facing manslaughter charges had taken its toll.

Chris' latest episode had come a bit unstuck – he'd just recently had a go at a heart transplant operation on an eleven-year-old boy and it wasn't as successful as the team would have hoped. The parents were rather put out. 'How do you think I felt?' complains Searle. 'You watch a massive haemorrhage in full close-up and try to keep your sense of humour. Besides, it was a f★★★★★★ fiddly operation. Not just a question of bunging the organ in and that's that – you've got all those little bits and pieces like blood vessels, arteries and membranes to join up as well. And it didn't help being dragged on a pre-shoot bender the night before by a camera-crew who were into double vodkas, vindaloos and snorting a vast quantity of cocaine.

BBC 1

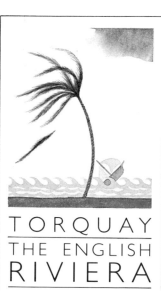

TORQUAY
THE ENGLISH
RIVIERA

10.00-10.01pm
A MINUTE'S PAUSE
This week, **Marmeduke Hussey** faces critics of overmanning at the BBC.
Research: LAURIE TOMPSETT. HENRY KINK. BELINDA COTTON. ANNABEL HUSSEY. DAVID FFRENCH-PPETERS. JUDY HARRODS.
Writers: ARCHIE TOOL. LINDA BOURNEMOUTH. JARVIS DORK. CRYSTAL NIMMO. GUNTER KARAJAN.
Studio Sound: JACK DUNKIN.
Film Sound: HARRY CASSETTE.
Design (Studio): BUNNY JIMPSON. NOEL FINCHAM. RED WELLIE.
Design: ZERO FEMFRESH.
FMs: LISA BROOM and DAVE PINKO.
PA: DORINDA PANTILE.
FA: MARCUS PROJECT.
Devised by: CANDIDA SMALLNESS.
Assistant to the Devisor: ANNE REGION.
Director: LORNA MUIRLY.
Assistant Director: GARETH FLUTE.
Direction Producer: KEITH BOREDOM.
Director in Chief: BENNO WALLIS.
Executive Director: CHRIS CRUMMY.
Producers: GEOFFREY POSSETT and BAZ VIM.
Production Associates: LUCRETIA STEROID. PAUL MAXWELL-HOUSE. GERTIE BELLOWS.
Production Director: SUE WATNEY.

Executive Producer: HUMBERT MOULE.
Co-Producer: TAMSIN DAY-LADDIE.
Assistant to the Co-Production: BRIAN TRESTLE.
Production Manager: TOMMY PROPS.
Production Editor: LINCOLN HANDKERCHIEF.
Series Producer: KEVIN JUNIOR-BUYER.
Produced by: FRED VALUE.
Assistant Editor: JIMMY GROPE.
Editor: WALLY STOAT.
Film Editor: JAMES DREWITT.
Executive Editor: BENNY CLUBMAN.
Series Editor: MARVIN BLOW-JOB.
Video Editor: WALDEMAR JUNKY.
Editor Editor: BARRY DOG-WALKER.
Editor in Chief: KENNETH GARAGE.
Technical Presentation: MARION MARION. LESLEY NORMAL.

10.02 DID YOU SEE
Ludovic Kennedy discusses *Right To Reply, Open Air, Network, Points of View, The Media Show,* with Robert Robinson, Anne Robinson and Muriel Gray and Bob Wellings.
Produced and directed by WILLIAM FLIPPER.

10.30 ACHMED AND JUNE
by COLIN BOSTOCK MOHAMMED
starring **Achmed Mohammed and June Achmed** *They Chop Hands Off, Don't They?* In which Achmed gets stoned, and June wonders how she will ever explain the bottle of whisky to the irate Mullah.
Designer: MOHAMMED ACHMED.
Director: MOHAMMED MOHAMMED.
Producer: MARTIN SHARDLOW.
Produced in association with the Iranian Broadcasting Corporation.

THOSE SLASHER TAPES IN FULL

THE OFFICIAL POLICE TRANSCRIPT OF THE HARROWING AND PAINFUL INTERROGATION OF THE EVIL MASS MURDERER DENNIS *"THE SLASHER"* FRAMBOZI BY TWO HONEST POLICEMEN, INSPECTOR REGINALD BRIBEASY AND SERGEANT ADOLPHE PORNO.

INSPECTOR BRIBEASY

SERGEANT PORNO   SLASHER

This is a direct unedited transcript. The speaker is indicated in the left-hand margin. The interrogation took place in a cell at Newham St Police Station.

BRIB: So,Slasher Frambozi...we finally meet up. You evil bastard Frambozi. I'm going to make mincemeat out of you and it's all going down on tape...'ere,Porno?

PORN: Yes,sir.

BRIB: AsxkkisxindkisixAre you sure this thing is working?

PORN: I pressed the button sir.

BRIB: There's no light on itXaKxX

PORN: I don't think it has a light sir.

BPIB: A^L l machines have lights don't they?

PORN: Not this one.

BRIB: Do you have to put money in it?

PORN: I shouldn't think so,sir. It's plugged in.

SLASHER: You've just got to make sure the record button is pressed at the same time as the play button.

BRIB: You stay out of this you murdering bastard.

SLASHER: O^N ly trying to help.

EPIB: Are you sure there's some film in it.

PORN: You don't need film in it,sir.

BRIB: Funny gadget!

SLASHER: You're an idiot Bribeasy.

BPIB: You shut up or l'll have you arrested.

PORN: He's already arrested sir.

BFIB: So,he won't be expecting it a second time on the same day!

PORN: Let's check if this tape machine is working... I'll just press this...
LOUD HIGH PITCHED SQUEAK ON TAPE...

BRIB: ...like they used to.

PORN: Say something into the mike.

BRIB: What mike?

PORN: It's that little hole there.

PRIB; I've been knocking me pipe-ash down that hole.

PORN: Say something for level.

BRIB: Testing testing...1 2 3 4 5...what's after five

PORN: 6

BRIB: 6666666 testing.

PORN: Right,I'll press rewend and play it LOUD LONG HIGH PITCHED SQUEAK.

BRIB: ...just not recording.

PORN: I'll go out and get some new batteries the,., Sir.

A DOOR OPENS AND CLOSES. FOOTSTEPS FADING.

BRIB: As soon as we get this tape-recorder working Frambozi I'm going to demolish you wьth words and drag a confession out of you.

SLASHER: Look,the tapex's still going round.

BRIB: I'm not falling for that.

SLASHER: N o,it is honest. It's probably recording everything we're saying

BRIB: S hut up yov.I don't want to hear another word out of you. Alright!?
TEN MINUTES SILENCE.FAINT PACING UP AND DOWN NOISES.
What's that slight whirring sound.

SLASHER: It's the tape machine.

BRIB:(VERY LOUD AND SLIGHTLY DISTORTED)You're right...th tape is going rounu...look there it goes... round and round...yes,there it goes again...Hey it's good isn't it. It's like a mini merry go round.Only without the painted horses,of course

A DOOR OPENS

PORNO: Batteries sir.I'll just take the back off.

XXIN A LOUD SHRIEK.SILENCE.SOME SCUFFLING.MORE SILENCE.WE HEAR A NEW VOICE.IT IS THE POLICE DOCTOR.

DOC: ... ...especially dangerous when it's plugged into the mains.

BRIB: He was just trying to get the tape machine started,Doctor. Is it serious?

DOC: Is he left handed?

BRIB: I don't know.

DOC: Did he play the violin?

BRIB: I don't think so.

DOC: He won't Be able to do much point duty from no on.
LOUD CRACKLE.

```
BRIB:     So how long do you think it's been off?

PORN:     I don't knowx sir.It's a 1 hour tape and it's
          about a quarter used.

BRIB:     But I've been questioning him with penetration
          and brilliance f for about 16 hours.

PORN:     It'sprobably not on the tape then sir.

BRIB:     Oh that's (EXPLETIVE DELETED) brilliant.Is the
          tape on now Sergeant?

PORN:     Er...let's have a look(CRACKLE)...No.

BRIB:     So It's not recording now then?

PORN:     No.sir.

BRIB:     Good.then just clear off and leave us alone
          for a few moments.I'm going to break this
          (EXPLETIVE DELETED)

          DOOR CLOSING

          You're a nasty (EXPLETIVE DELETED) Frambosi.

SLASHER:  Cut that out Bribeasy.Look down here under the
          table.

BRIB:     My God,one of your trouserx legs is rolled up..
          Good Lord...you're not...

SLASHER:  Course I am.

BRIB:     You should have said earlier.Here put this
          raincoat over your head we'll smuggle you out.

SLASHER:  That's very good of you.

BRIB:     Don't be silly...you know what we say at the
          lodge! Tok,tok wogga wogga..bindi bandi boo.

SLASHER:  Of course.What about the tape machine?

BRIB:     Oh leave that.Nobody here knows how to work it
          anyway.

SLASHER:  Come on then.

BRIB:     And XXX besides if they do find it out how to
          play it back they'll only be interested in
          deleting all the fucking expletives.
```

HE FINALLY CRACKS! BRIBEASY GIVES IN
AND ACCEPTS THE MONEY

News in brief

Briton killed in Earthquake

A British man was killed yesterday in what an eye witness called 'the worst earthquake ever seen in Bolivia'. Around 800 Bolivians also died.

Beirut bomb

A Briton was injured in yesterday's bomb in a Beirut hotel. Other people affected were all foreigners, but among the dead were, in order of importance: one American, two Germans and a Frenchman. The latter was in the bar at the time, probably drinking Pernod, and almost certainly couldn't be bothered to learn English, so the nasty foreign git had it coming.

British man hurt

Yesterday a British man was slightly hurt by a remark made about the cut of his suit in a Milan bar. He was comforted by his wife on his return to Gatwick Airport this afternoon. More pictures and full interview on centre pages.

Briton killed

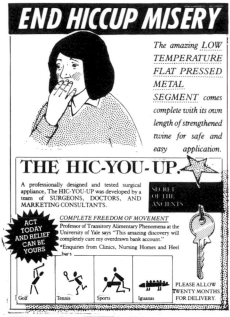

Obscenity (Miscellaneous Provisions) Act 1989

An Act to amend the law relating to obscenity; to extend the controls over the public display of offensive material; and for connected purposes.

[31st March 1988]

Be it enacted by the Queen's most Excellent Majesty, by and with the advice and consent of the Lords Spiritual and Temporal, and Commons, in this present Parliament assembled, and by the authority of the same, as follows:–

PART I

DEFINITION OF OBSCENITY

1.—(1) On such day as the Secretary of State may appoint by order made by statutory instrument the following matters shall for the purposes of this Act be defined as obscene and thenceforth be subject to the controls on obscenity and the public display of offensive material –

Regional accents on television before 9 pm; pro-celebrity golf matches; the basement lavatory in the Taj Mahal New Tandoori Restaurant, Holloway Road; tops of fat men's bottoms exposed by badly fitting jeans; Paul Daniel's height; Smiley stickers; people standing on the left on London Transport escalators; tampon adverts; Wayne Sleep; rolled-up jacket sleeves; films by Derek Jarman; Russell Grant, Russell Davies; anyone else called Russell; Ken Russell's ego; Bailey's Irish Cream; happily settled homosexual couples with *exactly* the same moustaches; happily settled *heterosexual* couples with exactly the same moustaches; that series of advertisements for Renault 25 with the smug couple and end lines like 'Don't you think you are being a bit hasty'; situation comedies written by Colin Bostock-Smith; sunglasses hooked down the front of shirts; drama students; Marti Caine in silver lurex dresses; Frankie Vaughan's porcelain cello; mime artists performing in the street before nightfall; the man in lager adverts with short hair, a thin tie and a not quite cockney accent; Richard Branson's teeth, beard and pullover; the personal problems of the members of Boy George's immediate and extended family; *Nuclear Power No Thanks* stickers in languages other than English; Terry Wogan's wig; the political opinions of the cast of EastEnders; stone cladding; any further book about the Bloomsbury Group; any further sections of the *Sunday Times;* Robert Maxwell's midriff; Lloyd Grossman's voice; caravans; personalized number plates; Happy Eater restaurant signs; Robert Robinson's haircut.

AT LAST, ALL ON THE ONE RECORD

FOOTBALL TERRACE FAVOURITES

Emlyn Hughes says, 'I think K Per have done brilliant. They have . . . they've done great . . . they really have done magic . . . I don't care what Mick Channon says . . . if this isn't the best football record in the world then I'm not Emmylou Harris . . . or something like that.'

K-per

INCLUDING . . .

'WHO'S THE WANKER IN THE BLACK?'
    by the Shed at Chelsea

'YOU COULDN'T SCORE IN A BROTHEL'
    by the Kop

'WE THOUGHT YOU WAS SHIT.
WE WAS RIGHT'
    by the Mile End Mob

André Previn says, 'A lot of people often say to me, "How come you've got a French name and an American accent, you smarmy little whining git? And what do you know about football anyway?" Well, I'm a true British citizen and therefore I love soccer and listening to this marvellous album just made me want to be standing there on the terraces at Lords, cheering Blackburn Rovers on to yet another great victory in the Cheltenham Gold Cup.'

'WHAT THE FUCKIN' 'ELL WAS THAT?'
    by Diana Ross and the Supremes

'WHO'S THAT LYING ON THE RUNWAY?'
    by the Leeds Boot Boys (live at Manchester)

'COME ON, THE TOWN'
    a duet by all Luton's supporters

'DOES SHE TAKE IT IN THE MOUTH?'
    the Peter Shilton Fan Club

'THERE'S ONLY ONE TEAM IN LONDON'
    by someone who doesn't know much about football

and many many more . . .

£5.99

AVAILABLE IN CD/CASSETTE

Any weekend in late summer, early summer or any of the other seasons. AT A LARGE THEATRE IN LONDON.

In aid of The London Palladium Overtime Fund and Sunshine Holidays for Freelance Television Technicians

A host of familiar faces and even more familiar sketches' faces in an...

AMNESTY

FOR ALL THAT OLD MATERIAL
(Just hand it in and no questions asked.)

FEATURING...

ROWAN ATKINSON in something from *Not the Nine O'Clock News*.

LENNY (Theophilus B. Wildebeest the Twenty-Fifth) HENRY.

MEL SMITH and GRIFF RHYS JONES reworking some duff old chat.

The unstoppable BILLY CONNOLLY not stopping.

JOHN CLEESE, hilariously failing to turn up again.

ERIC IDLE lives in California.

MICHAEL PALIN and TERRY JONES dust off an antique.

JASPER CARROTT doing insurance claims with a different jacket on.

FRY and LAURIE give Shakespeare masterclass the kiss of life.

ALAN BENNETT revisits his uncanny impression of a Northern Woofter.

RICK MAYALL and the Elephant's Nob joke.

BEN ELTON with some brand new stuff, like the old stuff.

ALEXEI SAYLE doesn't do this sort of thing any more.

RICHARD DIGANCE sings NEIL INNES.

The Secret Policeman's further pun on testicles

For the benefit of MARTIN LEWIS.

SELLE

JANUARY 1989

DIOR

ASPREY

CHARLES OF THE RITZ

GARRARDS

ESTÉE LAUDER

CONRAN

CHANEL

VAN CLEEF AND ARPELS

HERMES

CARTIER

BIGGEST EVER

Number of pages of adverts

BEST YET

This month we've finally managed to have no real articles at all

ALL YOUR FAVOURITE FEATURES

The two girls' bums advertising sun tan cream, what they are flogging in Selfridges at the moment, unnecessarily expensive french perfume, phallic lipsticks

FF 33.00
4.50
Germany DM 7.50
Australia $A 4.95
money will do

1.20

Sickness and Invalidity Benefit Claim Form

SIB

1 | Yourself *What?*

PLEASE USE BLOCK LETTERS *Wassat mean luv? OH! GOTCHA!*
If you can't fill this form in yourself, ask someone else to do so and to sign it
for you. *CHEEKY BUGGER, LET ME TALK TO A MAN...*

Surname: Mr/Mrs/Miss/Ms *I DUN ME FOOT.*
First names *I SAID - I DUN ME FOOT AND ITS KILLIN ME!*
Address *WOTS WRONG WIV YOU GIRL? I SAID I DUM ME*
BLEEDIN FOOT!!! Postcode *SOD THAT!*

Date of birth | *AINT* | *WIV* | *YA!* |

National Insurance number | *LOOK,* | *MY* | *KIDS* | *ARE* | *RUNNIN* |

STAFF/CLOCK/WORKS NUMBER | *ABOUT WIV THERE ARSES HANGIN OUT* |

2 | Details of sickness

Give details of your sickness. Words like
'unwell' or 'illness' are not enough ↖
WOT ABOUT WORDS LIKE FOOT?

Please say briefly why you are unfit to work *FOOT BLEEDIN FOOT!*

I DUN IT! SO ME, THE MISSUS AND ME KIDS ARE
ALL RUNNIN ABOUT WIV OUR ARSES HANGIN OUT!!!

■ Is your sickness due to an accident which happened while you were
working for any employer? *LOOK, JUST LET ME TALK TO*
SOMEONE HIGHER UP - A BLOKE
OR SUMMINK, WILL YOU DARLIN
I JUST WANT SOME BLEEDIN MONE

TICK ONE BOX | YES ☐ | NO ☐

■ Well you won't get no bleedin money till you answer a few bleedin
questions! Is your sickness due to an accident which happened while
you were working for any employer?

TICK ONE BOX | YES DARLIN ☑ | NO DARLIN ☐

■ That's more like.... Mr..er...? | Yourself *NOBBY CLARK.*

FORM SIB

Record-Breaking Figures

THE THOUSAND-YEAR REICH-OFF

Combined Service of Thanksgiving and Annual General Meeting of World War Two Inc (UK) PLC.

As the sirens wailed out once more over London, a packed meeting of shareholders, Nazi war criminals and warwishers came to pay annual tribute to 'Possibly the oldest and deadest horse ever to be flogged in the history of the world.'

As Joe Loss led the Regimental Band of the Death's Head Panzer Division into Glen Miller's theme from *The Charmer*, John Boorman and the cast of *Hope and Glory Two – Mother of the Free* – led the jitterbugging up the platforms, and the cast of *Winnie* sang hits from Howard Goodall and Herman Goering's smash flop, *Girlfriends*.

Bill Cotton asked for a minute's silence to think up a better idea than 'Wish Me Luck' for the autumn schedules.

But there was a muffled cheer as a straggling column of the survivors of *Tenko* and *Colditz* marched bravely across a 'Bombsite' specially created for the occasion by the Dockland Development Corporation.

They listened, biting back the tears, as Dame Edna Thompson and Sir Kenneth Brannagggh read movingly from Book One, Episode One of *'Ello 'Ello*.

'Oh, What a Lovely World War Two'

To the strains of *Theme from a Film too Many*, Sir Richard Attenborough himself then bounded onto the podium. He wiped a tear-stained face with a generous helping of engine oil and called attention to the finer attributes of 'That sprightly warhorse, the Holocaust.'

'My dears, from the days when I was just a novice, drowning in submarines, to the last few years when I have been lucky enough to become one of the overpaid hasbeens standing in the background of the 'brass hat' scenes, it has been a great, great comfort to me that there's always good old

World War Two to fall back on when the ideas get a bit thin, eh, loves?'

There were muffled 'Ayes!' from the Regiment of Veteran Programme Controllers, and then the reedy tones of the 'Force's Sweetheart', Sir John Gielgud, echoed around the bomb-scarred vaults as he led the faithful in prayer.

'Our Father,
Who art in Hounslow.
What did you do
In *The Fortunes of War*, Daddy?'

Deutschland über Dallas

All eyes now focussed on the bent and shrivelled figures of those who gave their all.

Jeremy Kemp, Anton Diffring, John Mills and Jack Hedley hobbled forward. Choking back the brandy, they laid wreaths in memory of 'those who had mugged

Canon Globus' stunning reconstruction of the Battle of El Alamein

Also present The Butcher The Baker The Candlestickmaker and The Right Bastard of Treblinka

and in reverse order the winners of the Best Uniform Competition . . .

Bidding is brisk for
the sale of the last
known self-portrait
of Adolf Hitler

before': the cast of *Dad's Army*; the Kenneth More Impersonation Squad; The Brigade of Noel Coward Soundalikes; and Sam Kydd.

'At the going-down of the credits, we shall remember them'

Next', in a tribute to the fallen warriors of the French Resistance, David Croft and Jeremy Lloyd danced around, their trousers round their ankles, waving their repeat fees from *It Ain't Half Over Mum*.

From atop a heap of unsold copies of Spike Milligan's classic *Hitler: His Part in my Bank Balance*, the manly tones of Professor Norman Stone suddenly cut through. Wiping the froth from around his toothbrush moustache, he castigated the 'Yobboes of Channel 4' for failing to make decent moving pictures about guns and things.

There was a short interruption from Count Nikolai Tolstoy, who rose to protest that nobody was paying any attention to his latest revelation that Joseph Stalin was, in fact, Winston Churchill with a false moustache, before a hush fell on the company.

'Publish and be bombed'

A sudden thundering of suede shoes marked the entrance of the massed legions of London Publishers. They reverentially laid copies of *Dachau Days*, *Belsen, Hospital Wing*, and *Lots of Gorgeous Black Uniforms and Huge Tanks* on the mile-high heap of remainders in the booking office.

Their leader, Brigadier Michael Fishwick (Fontana) expressed general thanks to the long serving members of MI5, SOE and Ultra for saving up a 'huge lump of old war stories until now'.

To cheers, he announced that 'Lieutenant' Rupert Murdoch had just bought the world syndication rights to *The Secret Diaries of Deirdre Frank Aged 16½* by Sue Townsend. 'It will stand alongside *Winston Churchill's Shaving Brushes, Illustrated*, *Bombs in my Begonias — the War Diary of Percy Thrower*, and *A Passage to South America* as the foundation of the industry for now and the foreseeable future.'

The Managing Director of World War Two Inc., Gunner 'Tommy' Mills-Grenade, Editor of the *Sunday Express*, rose to sum up. 'Martin Boorman is alive and well and living in South America making the *Emerald Forest Two*,' he intoned.

'Ladies and gents, the Second World War will never lie down, believe you me. What a great year! The head of Marketing, Kurt Waldheim, has just turned down fifty big ones for his memoirs. The *Of War* package has been selling like hot meat-

coupons. We've already had *Winds*, *Fortunes* and *Dogs*. We've got *Ravages*, *Turmoils* and *Spoils* up the spout, and we haven't even started with *Hamsters* and *Auberons*.'

To wild cheering, the minutes of the last meeting were authenticated by Lord Dacre, and the entire company repaired to the Grill Room of the Savoy for lashings of powdered egg and Wooton pie.

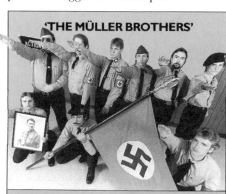

THE AYUSHI XL20 STEREO SYSTEM

THE XL20 is the very latest model from Ayushi (apart from our other very latest models – the XL30, XL40 and the XL3,425,947). Treat your new XL20 with care. It is a unique machine. It is a well-known fact that every stereo system sounds different. Of course, they do sound identical if you are playing the same album or tape – but generally there's a world of difference. Just listen to Beethoven on one system and then the Clash on another – you'll see what we mean.

Mains Lead Plug

The wires in the mains lead are coloured in accordance with the following code:

- **BLUE** — Neutral...or is that live?
- **BROWN** — Live...or Neutral, depending on whether it is or it isn't.
- **YELLOW/GREEN** — Earth...definitely... I think.

Guarantee

We guarantee to fix your system
a) if we can be bothered
b) if you manage to find our Service Depot
c) and thereafter, if you are able to get through on the phone

However, this guarantee expires exactly one day before you have any trouble at all with the system.

Warning
Watch out behind you.

What Do All The Buttons Do?

See diagram below.

On/Off Straightforward. On for on, and Off for off.

Tone Bit more complicated. Stick to On/Off or Volume.

Graphic Equalizer A device to help you if your graphics fall behind. Twiddle these, and your graphics will soon catch up. If things go well – they may even nose in front. Who knows? I know I don't.

TAPE Tape. (Not Leonard Cohen, remember.)

DOLBY B/DOLBY C The Dolby B and Dolby C have, of course, replaced the rather outmoded Dolby A, which was too old, and consequently not new enough. B, of course, stands for Button. C...doesn't. Basically the Dolby is a sophisticated device which allows you to listen to your system with the little green light on or off. Invaluable, especially for people addicted to little green lights.

Dubbing Button The dubbing button is used specifically for playing foreign tunes. The music is anglified, thus making it more accessible to the English ear. Plug your stereo into your TV and you can listen to Tchaikovsky with sub-titles. Incredibly modern and technical...and things.

Volume Basically the volume control controls the volume. What could be simpler?... Henry Kelly, for one.

LW Long Wave. Radio, basically. Radio 4 mainly. Deathly dull.

MW Medium Wave. Great button. Lots more stations. More pop music. Watch out for Radio 4 though.

FM/AM Eh...oh... AM for listening to the radio in the morning. FM...for listening in the afternoon. Should really be PM. Bad photograph.

PHONO Spanish for 'phone'. For those with EEC style phones can be very useful for... certain things.

AUX CD Auxiliary CD. A sort of back-up CD in case your main CD breaks down. I think the main CD is located round the back.

DSL Don't Say Leonard.

Mic Vol The guy that invented the whole shooting match. Good old Mic.

Mute Search Enables you to look for things in complete silence. Handy if your neighbours complain late at night.

Intro Scan A cheap gimmick turned into a crappy Radio 2 quiz game. Best ignored.

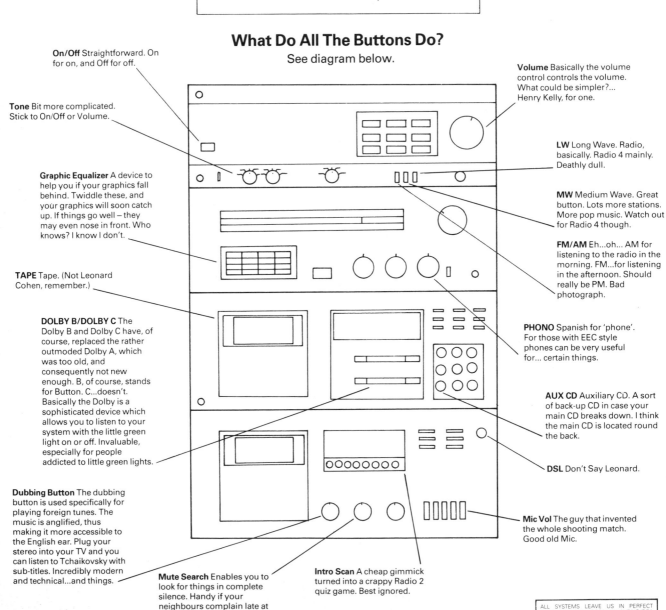

THE BRITISH SCHOOL OF MURDERING

PER CADAVRE VAUXHALL ASTRA

KILL THE EASY WAY WITH THE BRITISH SCHOOL OF MURDERING

ALL ASPECTS OF HOMICIDE COVERED INCLUDING

 • POISONING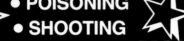
• SHOOTING
• 3-POINT TURNS ON MOTORWAYS

All the basic requirements of becoming a classic British Murderer.

Foundation course – everything you need to know about burial in the foundations of concrete bridge support.

Instructions given on the latest sawn-off shotguns or, if you prefer, an automatic.

Don't just leave it to luck. Make sure you know where to bury your victim so the body will be found a few months later by a couple of boys out playing.

ALSO

...get to know the theory and practice of chalk pits. Where are they, what are they and why are they always cropping up in real-life murder stories?

... Is avocado the best shade for an acid bath?

... pick which road to have associated with your crime... the A4, the A40 and the Great North Road already gone... still available: B67248 to B68340.

Learn how to get a reputation with your neighbours for being 'a bit of a loner'... 'Keeps himself to himself'... 'Mild mannered'... 'Very good to his mother, until he shot her'.

Discover the best way to wear that blanket over your head as you are taken into some godforsaken Magistrates' Court for the first of your many court appearances.

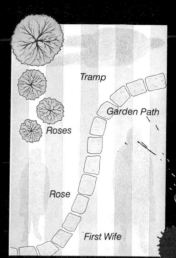

Plan your garden with the Nielsen-Christie method

Each student is assigned his own personal tutor. ▷

CID APPROVED

Just send the attached coupon to get the introductory murder package of your choice. Included in the package is a FREE map of Epping Forest, a copy of Pevsner's *The Shallow Graves of England and Wales* and a guide to South Coast Hotels

Graduation day

Please rush me a copy of one of your free GUIDES TO MURDER, *A Stab in the Dark*
I am interested in killing (please tick first preference)

MY WIFE	MY HUSBAND	MY LOVER	MY HUSBAND'S LOVER	8 OR 9 COMPLETE STRANGERS
☐	☐	☐	☐	☐

I am over 18 and have written this with malice aforethought

Signed _____

Alias _____

Address _____

_____

C.R.O. no. _____

Send to
BSM, the British School of Murdering,
FREEPARDON, 10 Rillington Place, London W10.

BSM

How The Face Of The East End Is Changing

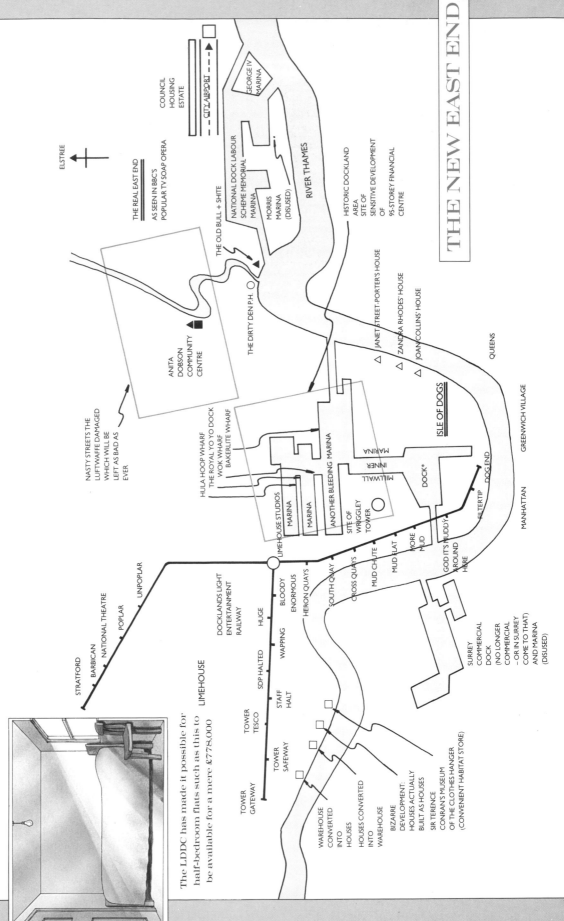

The LDDC has made it possible for half-bedroom flats such as this to be available for a mere £778,000

THE NEW EAST END

A (or the LDDC for short). The LDDC for short is a government Quango which has managed, amazingly, to inject new life into the Docklands by:

1 Handing out huge amounts of money to persuade companies to move into the area

2 Getting companies to move into the area by giving them huge amounts of money

3 Finding huge amounts of money and pumping them into any new company that will move into the area.

Amazingly, it has worked.

Centrepiece of the Docklands Development is to be Richard Roger's amazing 400-foot erection 'The Pink Giant' which he is planning to put up in the Isle of Dogs. This highly controversial project has excited comment from the moment the world-famous architect displayed a scale model of what he calls his 'handle on posterity' to a startled gathering in the City earlier this year:

'This monstrous carbuncle' Prince Charles

'Size isn't important' – Lady Antonia Fraser

'It will never stay up' – Joan Collins

'It's a penis, isn't it?' – Sir Hugh Casson

Richard Rogers is famous for his Lloyds Building and his Pompidou Centre in France.

'I built a lavatory cistern in Paris,' he says, 'and I see this as the next logical step.'

He shrugs off the criticism of his latest work. 'I bet Richard Seiffert could never pull off something as big as this . . . I see this project as an extension of my inner self. It's more than just a building. It's symbolic of what architects like me are trying to do to cities all over the world . . . It's big, it's brash, it's vibrant, it has a sense of humour.'

'It stinks,' responds fellow architect Richard Seiffert. 'And quite frankly, once it's been up for a while it will bore people stiff.

'And anyway, it isn't as big as all that. You wait 'till you see the whopper I'm sticking up on the South Bank. Then we'll see who the real man is around here.'

But Rogers is unrepentant. Already Christo, the Modern Event Artist, has plans to wrap it in plastic for the Tate.

An action committee of local residents had only one thing to say about the Wriggley Tower Development – 'Sod the Tower; when's Anita Dobson returning to EastEnders?'

Local East End Trader breaks into the Yuppie Market

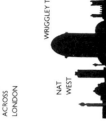

NAT WEST

ST PAUL'S

WRIGGLEY TOWER

TOWER BRIDGE

THE VIEW ACROSS LONDON

THE WRIGGLEY TOWER

VIEWING POINT

LIGHTNING CONDUCTOR + FLASHING LIGHT (WARNING TO AIRCRAFT)

INFLATABLE DOME

PRESTRUCTURAL BREEZEBLOCK SKIN

REVOLVING RESTAURANT

OUTSIDE LIFT SHAFT

BALL ROOMS (ONE SLIGHTLY LARGER THAN THE OTHER)

PLEASURE GARDENS

PINK GRANITE FACING

TREES, GORSE BUSHES AND UNDERGROWTH IN PUBLIC PARK

END HASTILY SCRIBBLED NOTE MISERY WITH NEW ANSA-DOOR

① ★MODERN micro-chip technology has created a truly astonishing device which will react automatically to the ring of the bell OR a knock on the door.

Its built-in megaphone projects your own ANSA-DOOR message through any standard letter-box.

Then your visitor simply has to shout back his or her own message.

The ANSA-DOOR records it for you to hear as soon as you get in.

NEVER AGAIN BE 'LEFT IN THE DARK' ABOUT ...

- friends dropping in for a chat
- the delivery man bringing the sofa-bed you've had on order for six months
- the gas man trying to read the meter
- neighbours asking you to join Neighbourhood Watch

PLUS the revolutionary **ANSA-DOOR** can be programmed to respond in special ways to specific callers. Up to ten separate **KEY PHRASES** will activate an individualized reply.
For example:

KEY PHRASE	REPLY
Summons	They've gone away
Double glazing	We've had it already...Yes, and patio doors...No, I'm not interested in stone cladding
Jehovah's Witness.....................	I'm not in. I have gone to the transfusion centre to donate blood
I'm a burglar	I'm just unchaining the Dobermans
We wish you a Merry Christmas, ... Merry Christmas, Merry Christmas, we wish you a Merry Christmas and a Happy New Year	Bugger off, we're Jewish

②

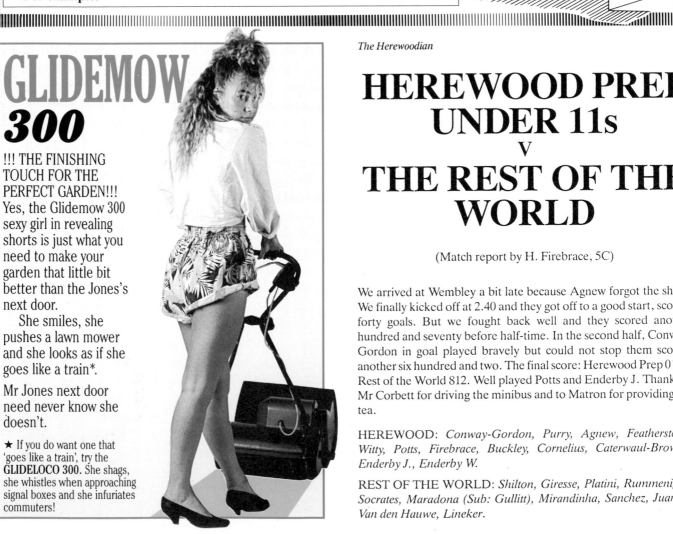

GLIDEMOW 300

!!! THE FINISHING TOUCH FOR THE PERFECT GARDEN!!!
Yes, the Glidemow 300 sexy girl in revealing shorts is just what you need to make your garden that little bit better than the Jones's next door.

She smiles, she pushes a lawn mower and she looks as if she goes like a train*.

Mr Jones next door need never know she doesn't.

★ If you do want one that 'goes like a train', try the **GLIDELOCO 300**. She shags, she whistles when approaching signal boxes and she infuriates commuters!

The Herewoodian

HEREWOOD PREP UNDER 11s
v
THE REST OF THE WORLD

(Match report by H. Firebrace, 5C)

We arrived at Wembley a bit late because Agnew forgot the shirts. We finally kicked off at 2.40 and they got off to a good start, scoring forty goals. But we fought back well and they scored another hundred and seventy before half-time. In the second half, Conway-Gordon in goal played bravely but could not stop them scoring another six hundred and two. The final score: Herewood Prep 0 The Rest of the World 812. Well played Potts and Enderby J. Thanks to Mr Corbett for driving the minibus and to Matron for providing the tea.

HEREWOOD: *Conway-Gordon, Purry, Agnew, Featherstone Witty, Potts, Firebrace, Buckley, Cornelius, Caterwaul-Browne Enderby J., Enderby W.*

REST OF THE WORLD: *Shilton, Giresse, Platini, Rummenigge Socrates, Maradona (Sub: Gullitt), Mirandinha, Sanchez, Juanito Van den Hauwe, Lineker.*

THE ANDERTON – GOD INTERVIEW

RECORD OF INTERVIEW

STATION ....

Room ....

Interview of (suspect's name) .... GOD

Date of birth .... 4,600 years BC

Interview by .... Chief Constable James Anderton

Date ....   Time commenced ....

Other persons present .... D.C. Michael Angel (recording)

Time ended ....

.... Holy Ghost (solicitor)

Q   Now, the first thing I have to do is to remind You that You are not obliged to say anything, but anything You say will be taken down and used in evidence.   Do You understand?

A   No reply   G

Q   Of course, You understand everything.   Please forgive me, it's just a formality.

A   No reply   G

Q   I don't know about the way of the world.   There seems to be a falling-off in moral behaviour, a lowering of standards. What on Earth can be done about it?

A   No reply   G

Q   It's very difficult to say, isn't it?

A   No reply   G

Q   Is there any guidance You can offer...   Any suggestions about what I can do to make things better?

A   No reply   G

Q   Well, it's very gratifying to think there is nothing You would like me to do that's any different.   You would say if You thought I was going down the wrong path ...

A   No reply   G

Q   Fine, fine.   I must say I am always helped by our little chats...   Now, to slightly less pleasant matters... Where were You on the night of the 17th of March?

A   No reply   G

Q   What do You know about the fire at Stalker's Warehouse - five million pounds' worth of property destroyed.   To say nothing of the deaths of two nightwatchmen and three firemen, twenty-five streets evacuated, an explosion wreck- ing fifteen homes.   A little bird tells me You might have had a hand in it, God.

A   No reply   G

Q   Come along now.   I might as well tell You that I have a report here that clearly describes the lightning bolt, which started it all, as an 'Act of God'.   Insurance job was it?

A   No reply   G

Q   Were you there?

A   No reply   G

Q   Of course You were there.   I know You were there, You know You were there.   Because we both know You are omnipotent AND omnipresent.   So it's no good if You try to come up with an alibi, is it?

A   No reply   G

Q   Just give me something to go on.   Help me so that I can help You.

(The suspect then said something in a still small voice which was unfortunately so still and small as to be inaudible.)

Q   Come along, I'm trying to do You a favour.   I'm taking a risk on Your behalf.   People say I'm mad to even talk to You.

A   No reply   G

Q   Well, there's obviously no point in continuing this inter- view.   I'll speak to You later on when You are prepared to behave more rationally.   Meanwhile, will You please initial each answer to show that this is a true record of the in- terview?

JOIN THE BEIRUT NEIGHBOURHOOD WATCH

Jan 2nd

Alias
Dear Moll Smith and Grief Jones,
c/o ~~The British Broad~~ The B.B.C.

I liked it when you was cow boys anyway
this is my idea for one of your skits.
What if Moll was pretendin to be a docter.
and Grief was pretendin to ~~be~~ a paishent
You could do all sorts of funny things.
                        Yours Sinsirly
                    ~~Brain~~ Brian Coooper.

P.S Give me regards to ~~The British~~
~~Broads~~ B.B.C.

(P.S. I dont want no mony for
this idea.)   xxx

Jan 10th

Alias
Dear Moll Smith and Grief Jones,
Its me agen — ~~Brain~~ Brian Coooper.

Ive had a bit of a think about that
skit idea I give you about Moll pretend-
-in to be a docter and Grief pretendin
to be a ~~pash~~ paishent and I think it
would be better if Grief was the docter
and Moll was the paishent instead.
What do you think?

                    Yours Sinsirly
                ~~Brain~~ Brian Coooper.
                        xxx

Febs 2nd

                Alias
Dear Moll and Grief,
    Some fuckers don it on the
telly last night! one bloke was
pretendin to be the docter and this
other bloke was pretendin to be the
~~paient~~ paishent! I was so anging I
Killed my missus and our kids and the
cats. If I find out you give them my
idea I will kill you too too you fuckin
Cowsons.

                Yours faithfuly
            ~~Brain~~ Brian Coooper

P.S You will not be hearing from me
agen and ~~les~~ less you did give
them my idea.

                    xxx

March 13th

Dear Mr Moll and Mr Grief,
I am ~~Brian~~ Brian Coooper's
solisiter and he says to me that
you give some other ~~blok~~ blokes his
idea about you doing a docter and
a paishent — he is livid! I am a verry
important solisiter and and less you
give my cliant $1000 youve had it!
And I'm not muckin about!

                    Yours Sinsirly
                ~~Brain~~ Jon Brown.

(P.S. I was thinking what if Moll was
a dentist and Grief was a policeman.
All sorts of funny things could
happen.)
                        xxx

(P.S I dont want no mony for this idea —
I get payd too much alreadys.)

THE WORLD OF
INFERIORS

MAY 1989 £14.10

PEACE AT LAST

WITH SAFE, EFFECTIVE

NESTLIDOWN
JUNIOR REMEDY

Contains: Aspirin, Sugar, Opium, Heroin, Morphine, Sherry, Gin, Valium, Cocaine, All Bran, Marijuana, Methylated Spirits, and a cosh for the baby.

GRRRRRR

DARE YOU DRIVE...

THE HOGGER: With its huge fat wheels, thing like a gate strapped on the radiator, enormous cowcatcher apparatus and twenty-five gears, the Bitsubatsu Hogger gives you the lot, with nobs on; particularly big, black, rugged nobs with bits of wire netting and impressive extra handles all over the place.

- *Ford the streams of Kensington.*
- *Climb the mountains of Docklands.*
- *Furrow the open plains of Barnes.*
- *Park with extreme difficulty anywhere in the centre of town.*

THE

Not so much a vehicle, more a big lump of tin with extra lights.

PETITION

To the Honourable Houses of Commons and Lords of Her Majesty the Queen Elizabeth's Government. We the undersigned hereby pledge our signatures to anything 'Right-On', whatever it may be, right. We strongly oppose anything uncool, like what her Majesty's Government proposes to do, right. (Anything pro nurses, old people or the freeing of animals bred only for their fur is *mega* Right-On, by the way.)

SIGNATURE	NAME	ADDRESS
Elta	BEN ELTON	C/O ELTON HOLDINGS. BARBADOS.
R. Coltrane	ROBBIE COLTRANE	ODDBINS, KILBURN HIGH ROAD.
Jimmy!	Jimmy Mulville	c/o Silver Fox, Fur Factory, Edmonton, Alberta, Canada
🐾	MAGOO	David Blunkett's dog
Rik	RICHARD MAYALL	61, THE KNOB, KNOB ST, KNOBBINGHAM GREEN KNOBLAND
Anderton	DETECTIVE CHIEF INSPECTOR JAMES ANDERTON	No 16, The right hand of God, Heaven, later Manchester
Henry Cooper	2 PINTS OF GOLD TOP	3 LOW FAT YOGHURTS (1 RASPBERRY, 1 STRAWBERRY AND ANOTHER RASPBERRY
Lofty	Tom "Lofty" Watts	c/o Islington Labour Party, Grange Street. n.1.
Major R. Ferguson	MAJOR RONNIE FERGUSON	c/o The Pink Pussy Club Dean St. W1
Lucan	LORD LUCAN	158, Grosvenor ... wait a minute. I'm not falling for that.
BOB	ROBERT GELDOF	c/o 37 Mind your own fuckin' business. ETHIOPIA.
R. Biggs	RONNIE BIGGS	'...' Sandaningo Rio de Janeiro
E. Hughes	EMLYN HUGHES	Don dun brilliant, 16 Acacia Road, Liverpool
David Steel	DAVID STEEL	'DUN SODALL' EAST STIRLING, FIFE
Runcie	ROBERT RUNCIE	XENON, 196 PICCADILLY
Derek Hatton	DEREK HATTON	Chez Guevara, Cred St., Liverpool 8
Benny	BENJAMIN "BENNY" GREEN	28 GRAHAM ROAD, HACKNEY, E.D. OLD BORO
Barry Took	BARRY TOOK	BED 78. THE JIM DAVIDSON HOME FOR THE CLINICALLY DEAD LITTLE DRIBBLINGS, EASTBOURNE
Nanette Newman	NANETTE NEWMAN	"The Simperings" Little Forbes, Hants
Richard Brien	Richard Brien	39 Acacia Ave, Sit com Land, Chea
Henry Cooper	SORRY! I THOUGHT IT WAS A NOTE FOR THE MILKMAN AND WHAT'S A SIGNATURE ANYWAY?	

THE *Slightly* IRRITABLE YOUNG MEN of the FIFTIES

CRITIC
VIVEAN MORTON
RECALLS
SOME EARLY
IMPRESSIONS.

JIMMY   Bloody hell, the sink's blocked again.

MARTHA   *(ironing)* Bloody typical. It's a waste of time phoning the bloody plumber if you ask me.

JIMMY   Too bloody right … they never turn up. Look at the state of this place… It's a disgrace.

MARTHA   I blame the Government.

(Act One Scene Two. *Look Back in a Bad Mood*)

The play, *Look Back in a Bad Mood*, was by a young playwright called John Upstart, who, with the poet Colin Pullover, was to form the nucleus of a radical new artistic movement known as The Slightly Irritable Young Men. Upstart managed to upset the whole literary establishment with his brash new style...

Upstart's often downright tetchy prose had a devastating effect. Grumbles and groans broke out in every corner of the literary community. Kenneth Tynan was one of the movement's more enlightened critics at the time:

As for J. Upstart's play at the Royal Court, the price of admission to this theatre has gone up to three and sixpence, and the seats are in an appalling state of repair … I don't know what they think they're playing at…
Tynan

People began to moan incessantly about everything, spurned on by the new literary vanguard who considered no aspect of British Life sacred. The Weather was mercilessly executed in Colin Pullover's famous poem, *Bloody English Weather*

Bloody English Weather
Bloody Hell
It's pissing down again
I'd move to Rio
If only the bloody publishers
Would advance me a few
Thousand…

It's almost impossible for us now to overestimate the impact of this play. To an audience raised on the British tradition of keeping a stiff upper lip,

NO ENGLISH PLAY HAD BEEN WITHOUT AT LEAST ONE SET OF FRENCH WINDOWS FOR OVER TWO HUNDRED YEARS. WHEN UPSTART'S FIRST 'FRENCH-WINDOWLESS PLAY' WAS STAGED, MANY FORESAW THE END OF THE BRITISH THEATRE.

 A CONTEMPORARY CRITIC DESCRIBES 'THE HUSH THAT DESCENDED OVER THE AUDIENCE' WHEN THE FIRST REAL 'DOOR' APPEARED IN AN UPSTART PLAY. UPSTART COMPOUNDED THE EFFECT BY REFUSING TO MAKE A SINGLE REFERENCE TO 'FRENCH WINDOWS' IN ANY OF HIS PLAYS.

THE ORIGINAL KITCHEN SINK AS IT APPEARED IN *LOOK BACK* IN 1956. FOR UPSTART, THE WHOLE EXPERIENCE OF BRITISH ANGST REVOLVED AROUND PLUMBING AND PLUMBERS. THIS UNIT SAW SERVICE THROUGHOUT HIS MOST CREATIVE PERIOD 1956-63.

The dress rehearsal of Samuel Beckets' play *Waiting for Godot* just before his radical re-write

WHERE ARE THEY NOW?

Thirty years on, a critic rediscovers the 'Irritables'. Are they still as irritating as ever or have they mellowed with age?

I found Colin Pullover attempting to annoy walkers on Hampstead Heath with his latest poem, *I Wouldn't Feed this Muck to a Pig*. Still writing, and still wearing the same suit, he is about to complete a new book, profoundly influenced by the experience of parenthood, entitled *What the Bloody Hell Time Do You Call This Then?* He replied to my suggestion that he was not as irritable now as he was in his youth by throwing small pellets of rabbit turd at me.

Upstart's present behaviour seemed initially more disappointing ... professing to be basically content with his life due to a lucrative deal on overseas sales of his plays. He was finally roused to his former passion on the subject of the faulty demister on the back window of his Volvo, on which he treated me to a seven-hour monologue…

CORE CURRICULUM POEM

With the Core Curriculum, education will be stripped down to its bare essentials. For example, it will no longer be necessary for children to study all the poems written in the English language. They will merely have to learn this Core Curriculum Poem which has been compiled from a recently published anthology of famous poems compiled and edited by myself.

CORE CURRICULUM POEM

I wandered lonely as a cloud,
To the lonely sea and the sky,
The noblest Roman of them all
Will know the reason why.

There's a breathless hush in the close tonight
(Capten, art tha' sleepin' there below?),
The time has come, the Walrus said,
I will arise and go.

April is the cruellest month
When icicles hang by the wall.
A man's a man for a' that,
Old Uncle Tom Cobley and all.

The King was in his counting house,
Drinking the blood red wine;
The ploughman homeward plods his weary way,
Oh World! Oh Life! Oh Time!

For East is East, and West is West,
Nor all that glisters, gold,
Should auld acquaintance be forgot
In the brave days of old.

Yours sincerely,

Kenneth Baker

Kenneth Baker

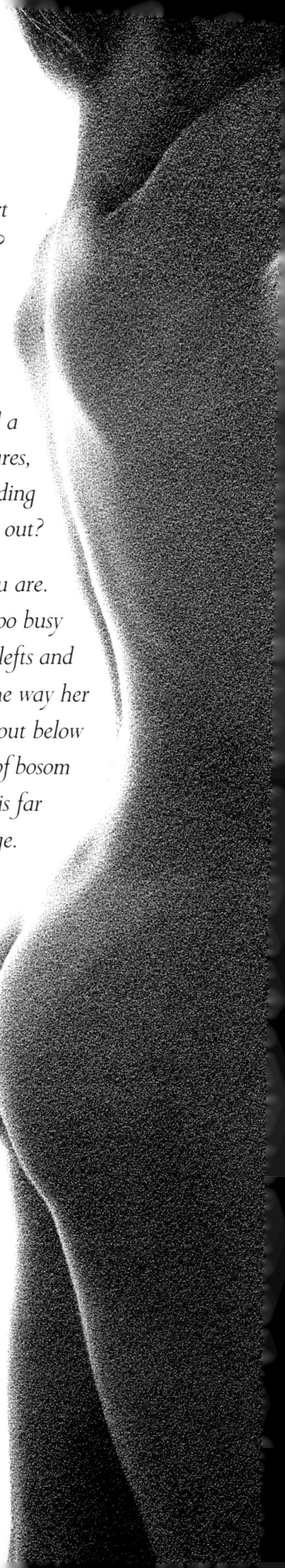

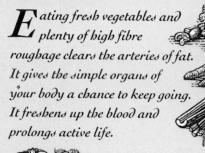*E*ating fresh vegetables and plenty of high fibre roughage clears the arteries of fat. It gives the simple organs of your body a chance to keep going. It freshens up the blood and prolongs active life.

If you don't watch out, you could end up living until you're a stupid old croak. The choice is yours. Lashings of creamy butter now, or years of gibbering dotage later. Thanks to yoghourt, a significant percentage of adult men and women now end up muttering in bus queues. Because of natural nut-bars, it's standing-room only on Eastbourne prom.

A recent medical report has proved that extended old age makes your clothes look too big for you.

Research has conclusively shown that you will live in Bexhill. You will think your children never come to visit you. And you will go 'tut tut tut'. You could even end up being endlessly lampooned in comedy magazines. Worst of all, you'll end up having nothing but other daft old bats for company.

Think about it, while you can still think. Eat fat, smoke fags and swill beer, or end up waiting for the tide to come in, covered in wrinkles.

Die nice and young.

You know it makes sense, and it costs us less.

Issued by
THE HEALTH EDUCATION QUANGO.

'I USED TO BE A MAN!!'

'IN FACT, I STILL AM! I JUST DRESSED UP IN THIS WOMEN'S UNDERWEAR TO GET MY PICTURE IN THE *NEWS OF THE WORLD*,' SAYS TV FUNNY MAN GRIFF RHYS JONES.

CONCALL

PHONE NOW 02 796 443 272 986. Twenty-four hour service.

PLEASURES OF THE EAST The weather in Scarborough and Hull.

BEDTIME SECRETS Getting the sofa bed open cleanly and quickly.

HOUSEWIFE FANTASIES Shake and Vac – the full story, plus the really satisfying snack you can eat between Cuppa Soups.

SCHOOLGIRLS Talk about ponies, pimples and ballet.

BIG BUSTS Detective Chief Inspector Bribeasy on raiding a block of flats in Tottenham.

DIRTY TALK Leslie Crowther looks at your understairs.

YOUNG CONSERVATIVE SUPPLIES

● Fat girls in taffeta dresses by the gross. ● Boxed bread rolls. ● Extra fizz, guaranteed thirty-foot range (as used by Grand Prix winners). ● 'Nuke Brent' stickers. ● Shiny dinner jackets. ● Matching sets of braying ninnies. YOUNG CONSERVATIVE SUPPLIES 'Brokers', Poofter in the Fountain, Gummerville, Surrey.

PRESENTS BY POST.

Take the wanting out of waiting.

'Sony Comaman'. The voice of Jimmy Saville rushed to your unconscious Loved One. Watch them jump up from their truckle and run screaming from the ward.

The perfect Valentine: a sheep's heart in a cardboard box, complete with white gristly bits. Offal by post. Allow ten days for decomposition.

Gift-wrapped Steradent for the geriatric in your life. Fizzmail. 01 222 22222.

As clean as a new pin! Banish dirty needle worries. A year's supply of tough, sparkling, unused needles in glittering Taiwanese steel, for the addict in your life. Phoneafix.

Instant relief from stress. The Dento-Chew miracle length of non-toxic plastic in the shape of a pen. Dr Freud writes: 'A Dento-Chew is a substitute nipple. Whenever the pain starts I simply reach for my Dento-Chew'. Only £11.50.

Old & Past It In Tinsel Town? Join the Hollywood Darby & Joan Collins Club. Luncheon, bingo and appearing in tatty soap operas gives continued hope to the elderly in the twilight of their years.

Sad, depressed, suicidal? Join EXIT, the club people are killing themselves to get into. Annual membership £10.00. Life membership £5.50.

JOB VACANCIES

EXPERIENCED CHEF required by soon to open Belgian restaurant. A knowledge of horses essential. Write Box No 25.

BRITISH NUCLEAR FUELS seek person to stick finger in leak at Sellafield plant. Would suit little Dutch boy.

BEST BOY required by Film Company. Duties: to explain why a Best Boy is required and what exactly he does. Suit man or woman of any age or any ability. Apply P. Bennet Jones, 1002 Expenses Mews, Soho.

● YOU ARE loquacious and outgoing. ● You live in Ilford or Upminster. ● You never go South of the River. ● Although you keep your political opinions to yourself you think Maggie's done a great job. ● You

are just what the London Taxi Service has hundreds of. Apply now and ride around London for two years with a clip board strapped to the front of your moped. Write in confidence to the Controller of Gabby Nonsense. I know it. It's Just up Here Somewhere Isn't It? No Such Place Mate. London.

HOW MUCH is your job worth? DOORKEEPERS required to make constant estimations. Write detailing previous bloody-mindedness to the Head of Bogus Uniforms, Plate Glass House, Thin Tash Crescent, London SW12.

● EXCITING OPPORTUNITIES. ● GREAT POSSIBILITIES FOR ADVANCEMENT. ● FANTASTIC REWARDS. ● RECOGNISE IT?? Of course not. Because it's the job you're doing at the moment! Get back to work, you lazy bastard, and stop looking over your shoulder in company time. Otherwise this ad will be appearing for real.

A JOB IN SALES £40,000 plus. Sell one of our plusses for £40,000 and make a mint.

HEAD HUNTERS UNLIMITED ● You are highly motivated. ● You are looking for new and exciting challenges. ● You are about five foot eight with receding hair and a blue pin-stripe suit with a shiny bottom. ● You left your briefcase in our office. Oh, and by the way, you haven't got the job.

EARN HUGE AMOUNTS OF CASH IN YOUR SPARE TIME. Up to £30,000 for next to nothing. We have a list of companies looking for non-executive directors prepared to rubber stamp any mad cap scheme we come up with. Including Napalmoco, the Cape Corporation of Lower Africa, Indian Refineries PLC, Big Tits Gaming Inc of America. Suit MPs, minor royalty, peers of the realm, high ranking members of the Services, retired Chief Constables etc, etc. Apply in confidence to His Royal Highness, Admiral The Duke of Bophal DSO, PO Box 46.

MEDIA OPPORTUNITY. A fast-growing media-based leisure company with interests in Hollywood films, Caribbean adventure holidays and celebrity management in the South of France, as well as South Sea Island windsurfing, fashion projects and worldwide rock music development seeks an alert, outgoing man or woman aged 20-25 to water rubber plants in Harlow Headquarters Building. No experience required. Apply 'Indoor Exotics Opportunity', Beige Tower, Harlow Industrial Estate, Harlow.

NCP. Highly motivated vehicular-emplacement, spatial area entry and exit control-function operative required. Must have at least one finger. Write to 'No Change Given', NCP House, Clamp St, South Mimms.

DIRECTOR GENERAL. We are looking for a new Director General to head the management of the best broadcasting system in the world. The successful applicant will: have spent the last five years in the position of Deputy Director General of a major public broadcasting corporation within the United Kingdom. Have experience in deputising for a Director General while he is away in New York, Hong Kong, Montreux etc. – Be prepared to travel to New York, Hong Kong, Montreux etc. – Wear a suit. – Have been promised the job five years ago. Apply in writing to The Chief Executive of The Broadcasting Commission. The successful applicant will know the address of the Chief Executive of the Broadcasting Commission.

THE MIDDLE OF NOWHERE EMIRATE OF THE GULF. Requires: A Director of the Royal Middle of Nowhere Hospital. A Deputy Director of the Royal Middle of Nowhere Hospital. Medical Chief of Staff of the Royal Middle of Nowhere Hospital. Matron of the Royal Middle of Nowhere Hospital. Architect of the Royal Middle of Nowhere Hospital. Builder for the Royal Middle of Nowhere Hospital. Patients for the Royal Middle of Nowhere Hospital. And while we're here: Manager for national football squad, miracle-working desert engineers, oil riggers, consultants, therapists, dancing girls. You name it. We're too rich to bother to do it ourselves and too boring to attract anyone to do it for us. Apply in writing to Sheik Abdul Al Nowhere, Royal Emirate of the Middle of Nowhere Recruitment Office, Shady Trees, Haslemere, Surrey.

IMPORTANT NOTICE:

Many thanks to all those who made our liver appeal such a success. The doctors at Haregrove Hospital would, however, like to speak to a Mr T. Harbinson, of Dorking, Surrey, who appears to have misunderstood the advert and may require urgent medical attention. Mr Harbinson, we've put it in the freezer compartment of Terry's fridge, but were not sure how long liver keeps. So please get in touch.

DEDICATION

This book is dedicated to the men and women of the Royal Naval Reserve w' through two World Wars selflessly and bravely gave of their all that the sea lanes mi; remain open. And, in particular, to the men of *HMS Brisket*, the which ship, w engaged in action with the enemy in the Baring Sea in April 1943, foundered with hands, so that vital supplies of weapons and ammunition might be convoyed to Ru in her hour of darkest need, and Hitler's legions of darkness be routed by the force good. Oh, and also my cat, Fergie.

WRITTEN BY:
Griff Rhys Jones and Clive Anderson

With additional material by Rory McGrath and Paul Smith/ Terry Kyan/Roger Planer/Robin Driscoll/Jamie Rix/Nick Wilton/Moray Hunter/John Docherty/Laurie Rowley/ Peter Fincham/Jonathan Crowe/Roland Paterson/ Rebecca Stevens/Paul B. Davies/James Hendrie/Simon Greenall/Chris Lang/Andy Taylor

DESIGN AND ART DIRECTION:

GRAHAM DAVIS ASSOCIATES
DESIGNERS: Graham Davis and Kevin Ryan
ASSISTED BY: Jorge Dager and Wayne Humphries

SPECIALLY COMMISSIONED PHOTOGRAPHY:

DAVID LEAHY
Assisted by Kirstie Sissons at JOHN PRICE STUDIOS

STILL LIFE: Duchess of Windsor Cutlery/Reader's Digest Condensed Novels/Alone to the Pole/Sunday Lunch/Designer Things/No Smoking/Eauverpriced
MODELS: Sassoon/Natural Childbirth/Health Warning/AIDS/Slasher Tapes/Glidemow/Peace At Last
MEL AND GRIFF: He's A Friend of Yours/Natural Childbirth/Problem Page/*Radio Tomes*/Slasher Tapes/I Used to be a Man/Economy Pack
COVER AND BACK COVER

ILLUSTRATIONS (in order of appearance)

ROB SHONE: *Harpies & Queens*/Spot the Difference/Natural Childbirth/*Slow Life*/Telbridge Keels/Stamps/Wondrous Gags/Time Share/Hallmark/Balls/Torquay/Hiccup/Hearing Aid/Inflatable Griff inserts/Stereo/BSM/East End/Ansadoor/Fifties
MARK ROGERSON: Kerpow!
CRAIG AUSTIN: Sassoon
CHRIS DAWSON: Duchess of Windsor Cutlery (models)
MIKE ROCKET: *Slow Life* (Jasper Conran)
SUSAN ALCANTARILLA: Alone to the Pole
DAVID LAWRENCE: Shakespeare
STEVE BIÈSTY: Air Traffic Controller Guide
TREVOR DUNTON: *Paunch*
GRAHAM THOMPSON: *Paunch* (after Bateman)/Hogger
MARK TAYLOR: Inflatable Griff
CAROLINE CHURCH: Health Food

ALL OTHER VISUAL MATERIAL:
Graham Davis/Kevin Ryan

PICTURE RESEARCH:
Mira Connolly

PHOTO LIBRARY CONTRIBUTIONS:
Ardea London Ltd/Peter Arkell/Aspect Picture Library/Associated Sports Photography/BBC Enterprises Ltd/BBC Hulton Picture Library/Mira Connolly Collection/EWA Picture Library/Gamma/John Garret/Sally and Richard Greenhill/Susan Greenhill/George Herringshaw and Associates/Robert Hunt Library/Hutchinson Library/Dafydd Jones/The Image Bank/Leo Mason/Bill McLaughlin/ Science Photo Library/Sipa Press/Frank Spooner Pictures/Spectrum Colour Library/Syndication International/TalkBack/Topham Picture Library/Popperfoto/Rex Features Ltd/Royal Court Theatre

SPECIAL THANKS TO:
Ceri/Howard Chandler/Gail Davis/Kerry Fuller/Murray Harris/Sue Henesy/Max McGonical/David McMillan/William Payne/ Colin Woodman
COSTUMES SUPPLIED BY:
BBC Costume Department
MAKE-UP BY: **WIGS:**
Jan Harrison Shell   Derek Easton

TYPESETTING:
Denzil Graphics

First published in 1988 by Fontana Paperbacks
8 Grafton Street, London W1X 3LA

Copyright © TalkBack Advertising Limited 1988

Printed and bound in Great Britain by
William Collins Sons & Co. Ltd., Glasgow